Chile

Chile

BY SYLVIA MCNAIR

Enchantment of the World
Second Series

Children's Press®

A Division of Grolier Publishing

NEW YORK   LONDON   HONG KONG   SYDNEY
DANBURY, CONNECTICUT

Frontispiece: Traveling by donkey cart near San Pedro de Atacama

Consultant: Jennifer Schirmer, Ph.D., Anthropologist and Lecturer on Social Studies at
Harvard University

Please note: All statistics are as up-to-date as possible at the time of publication.

Visit Children's Press on the Internet: http://publishing.grolier.com

Book production by Herman Adler Design Group

Library of Congress Cataloging-in-Publication Data

McNair, Sylvia.
      Chile / by Sylvia McNair.
          p. cm. — (Enchantment of the world. Second series)
      Includes bibliographical references and index.
      Summary: Describes the geography, plants, animals, history,
economy, language, religions, culture, sports, arts, and people of
Chile.
      ISBN 0-516-21007-6
      1. Chile—Juvenile literature. [1. Chile.] I. Title.
II. Series.
F3058.5.M46 2000
983—dc21   99-12689
                                                                          CIP

© 2000 by Children's Press®, a Division of Grolier Publishing Co., Inc.
All rights reserved. Published simultaneously in Canada.
Printed in the United States of America.
    2 3 4 5 6 7 8 9 10 R 09 08 07 06 05 04 03 02 01 00

Acknowledgments

The author wishes to give special thanks to Oscar Kolb, who was responsible for her first visit to Chile. She is also grateful to the government of Chile, which, through its department of tourism and the embassy in Washington, D.C., provided materials and assistance. Thanks as well to the office of the Chilean consul in Chicago. Finally, her gratitude goes to Anna Idol, who always reads her manuscripts and makes helpful suggestions.

Cover photo:
A young *huaso*

Contents

CHAPTER

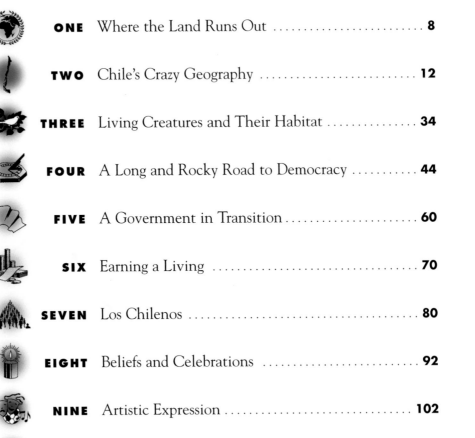

Dancing the *cueca*

An Andean folk
instrument

Where the Land Runs Out

A legend tells that after God finished creating the world, He found many things left over. There were lakes, mountains, rivers, forests, deserts, a slice of blue sky, and a big portion of the oceans. Not wanting to let all this beauty go to waste, He let it fall into a corner of the earth. That is how Chile was born.

LONG AGO, PEOPLE LIVING NEAR THE WEST COAST OF South America heard stories of a place far to the south where the land was broken up into thousands of little islands. They called it *Chile*, which meant "where the land runs out" in their language.

Chile is a land of fire and ice, of hot springs, volcanoes, and glaciers. It has the driest desert on earth in the north and endless ice-filled waters in the south. These natural barriers,

Opposite: **Osorno Volcano**

A cruise ship in front of the San Rafael Glacier in Patagonia

No part of Chile is very far from the vast Pacific Ocean.

Young people attending a festival in Santiago

plus high mountains to the east and a vast ocean to the west, separate it from the rest of the world. Chile's scenery is magnificent and unique. But, as if nature is never satisfied with its landscape, frequent earthquakes keep shaking things up and moving things around.

Most of Chile's people are descended from native Indians and Spanish settlers, with many other groups added along the way. Their culture, although heavily influenced by Spanish culture, is truly unique. The people are not Spanish, or Latin; they are *chilenos*—Chileans.

Chile has been struggling toward democracy for nearly 200 years. Along the way, it has experimented with socialism and has survived a harsh military dictatorship. Out of its problems have come great poetry, songs of struggle, and novels. The poetry of Gabriela Mistral and Pablo Neruda introduced the Chile of earlier times to the world. More recently, Violeta Parra's songs and Isabel Allende's novels have continued to tell Chile's story.

In today's modern world of fast travel and instant communication, Chile is no longer isolated from the rest of the world because of its mountains and seas. It is an important member of the family of nations. Let's get acquainted.

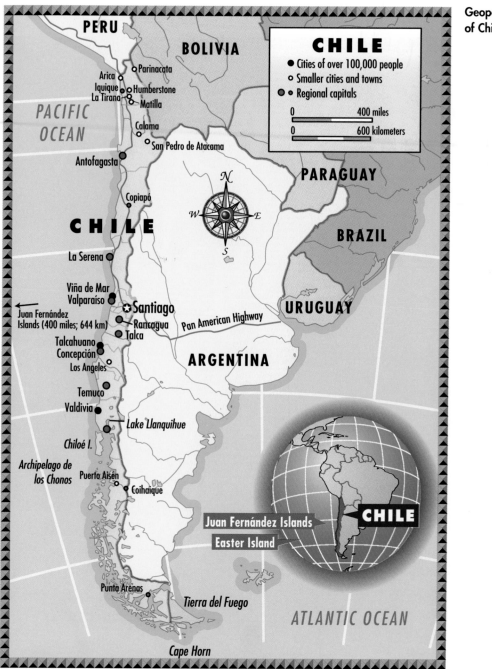

PERU

BOLIVIA

CHILE
● Cities of over 100,000 people
○ Smaller cities and towns
◉ Regional capitals

0   400 miles
0   600 kilometers

*PACIFIC
OCEAN*

Parinacata

Arica
Iquique
La Tirana
Humberstone
Matilla

Calama
San Pedro de Atacama

Antofagasta

PARAGUAY

Copiapó

C H I L E

N
W   *E*
S

BRAZIL

La Serena

Viña de Mar
Valparaíso

URUGUAY

☆ Santiago

Juan Fernández
Islands (400 miles; 644 km)

Rancagua
Talca

Pan American Highway

Talcahuano
Concepción
Los Angeles

ARGENTINA

Temuco
Valdivia

Lake Llanquihue

Chiloé I.

*Archipelago de
los Chonos*

Puerto Aisén

Coihaique

Juan Fernández Islands
Easter Island

CHILE

Punta Arenas

Tierra del Fuego

ATLANTIC OCEAN

Cape Horn

Chile's Crazy Geography

CHILE IS SHAPED LIKE A STRING BEAN. IT IS THE LONGEST and narrowest country in the world. One writer described its geography as *loca* (crazy), and Chileans enjoy using that description.

The world's driest desert is at the northern, tropical end of the nation. The land in the south is broken up into thousands

Opposite: **The Pacific coast in the north, near Antofagasta**

The Atacama Desert is the driest desert in the world.

of islands and has a sub-Antarctic climate, similar to much of Canada's. Some of the world's highest mountains and hundreds of volcanoes—fifty of them active—are in Chile. Easter Island, part of Chile, is 2,000 miles (3,219 kilometers) away from the rest of the country, in the Pacific Ocean. These are just a few of the unusual features of this nation's crazy geography.

All of Chile is south of the equator. In the Southern Hemisphere, seasons are just the opposite of those north of the equator. Spring begins in September, summer in December, autumn in March, and winter in June.

Chile has vast extremes in climate, from hot and dry in the north to cold, windy, and damp in the south. It never rains in some sections, while other sections have as much as 200 inches (508 cm) of rainfall a year. Climate and temperature also vary widely according to elevation. It can be blisteringly hot at sea level while wintry storms are blowing only a few hours' drive away in the mountains.

Stretching down the southwest coast of South America, Chile is 2,650 miles (4,265 km) from north to south and only 265 miles (427 km) from east to west at its widest point. So every spot in the nation is close to both the Pacific Ocean to the west and, except for the far offshore islands, the Andes Mountains to the east. The ocean waters are very cold along the entire coast because of the Humboldt Current, which flows north from Antarctica.

Three other South American nations share borders with Chile—Peru in the north, and Bolivia and Argentina in the

Chile's Geographical Features

Area: 292,135 square miles (756,571 sq km)

Largest City: Santiago

Highest Elevation: Nevado Ojos del Salado, 22,566 feet (6,878 m)

Lowest Elevation: Pacific Ocean, sea level

Longest River: Loa River, 275 miles (443 km) long

Lowest Average Temperature Range: 37°F–50°F (3°C–10°C), in Punta Arenas

Highest Average Temperature Range: 45°F–72°F (7°C–22°C), in Santiago

Lowest Average Annual Rainfall: 0.5 inch (1.3 cm), at Antofagasta

Highest Average Annual Rainfall: 200 inches (508 cm), near the Strait of Magellan

Number of Volcanoes: 1,080 (10% of the world's total)

Greatest Distances: North–south: 2,650 miles (4,265 km); east–west: 265 miles (427 km)

Amount of Temperate Rain Forest: 34,984,553 acres (14,158,248 hectares)

east. The Pacific Ocean forms the long western border. The southern border is the South Pole, where part of the continent of Antarctica is claimed by Chile.

Green fields below the Andes Mountains in Chile's Central Valley

Most of Chile's land rises from sea level in the west to the lofty Andes Mountains in the east. The slope upward goes through four distinct geographic zones. Each is long and narrow. The coastal strip gives way to the coastal *cordillera* (mountain range), then to the *pampa* (plain) or *altiplano* (high plain), and finally to the Andes.

From north to south, Chile's three major land regions are the Northern Desert, the Central Valley, and the Archipelago. They are strikingly different from one another.

The Northern Desert

Much of the northern half of Chile is desert. The Atacama Desert, called the *Norte Grande* (Great North) in Chile, is the driest desert in the world. It reaches from the Peruvian border on the north to the Aconcagua River, slightly north of the center of the nation. It never rains in most of the Atacama. A thick fog, called the *camanchaca*, often forms during the night, but the morning sun quickly burns it away. Scientists have created "cloud trappers," a method of capturing some of the moisture from the fog.

Major towns in the Atacama are along the seacoast—Arica, Iquique, and Antofagasta. Arica and Antofagasta are seaports. Without rain, nothing can grow in the desert, so farming is possible only in a few small oases—green, fertile areas. But there are riches under the soil—copper, nitrates, silver, and salt. Nitrates are salts that have been widely used in the manufacture of fertilizers and explosives; nitrate mining was once an important industry in Chile.

Copper ore from the Chuquicamata copper mine

La Cordillera de los Andes

La Cordillera de los Andes (the Andes Mountains) are the "spine" of South America. The range is fairly narrow, especially in Chile, but this mountain chain is one of the longest land barriers in the world. The range runs roughly parallel to the shore of the Pacific Ocean, all the way from the coast of the Caribbean Sea in Colombia in the north to Cape Horn in Chile, some 4,500 miles (7,242 km) to the south.

The highest peak in Chile is Nevado Ojos del Salado. It towers 22,566 feet (6,878 m) above sea level, east of Copiapó on the border with Argentina. Even in tropical Chile—the region north of Antofagasta—it is very cold in the high Andes. Lower mountains—under 3,000 feet (914 m)—in this region are called the *tierra caliente* (hot land). From 3,000 to 6,000 feet (914 to 1,829 m) is the *tierra templada* (temperate land), and from 6,000 to 10,000 feet (1,829 to 3,048 m) is the *tierra fría* (cold land). Above that is the snow line, where it is too cold for trees and most other vegetation to grow.

A number of ghost towns are scattered in the desert where miners once lived. One of the mining camps, Humberstone, is near Iquique. It is now completely deserted, but the houses, public buildings, and town swimming pool still exist. Near the small town of Calama is the largest open-pit mine in the world, the Chuquicamata copper mine.

One of the most amazing sights in the desert is the Valley of the Moon. Near the inland town of San Pedro de Atacama, it is an eerie landscape of salt crystals and colored gypsum and clay. Animal and plant life cannot exist in this strange, flat expanse of land.

Strange salt formations dot the Valley of the Moon.

**The geysers at El Tatio
erupt daily.**

Another natural wonder near San Pedro is the daily erup-
tion of some 100 geysers. It happens every morning, just before
sunrise, high in the Andes at El Tatio. Spectacular columns of
hot water and steam gush forth from the frozen earth. Some of
the spurting fountains look like mini volcanoes.

South of Antofagasta the desert is semi-arid, much less dry than the Atacama. This section is called *Norte Chico* (Small North). Grapes, other fruits, and vegetables are cultivated in valleys of the Norte Chico. Fishing is important all along the coast.

The Central Valley

Chile's Central Valley is the country's heartland. Most of the nation's agriculture and industry are concentrated in this region, and it is the most populated. Chile's four largest cities—Santiago, Valparaíso, Viña del Mar, and Concepción—are here.

The Central Valley is blessed with many rivers that are fed by icy waters from the snowcapped Andes. Major waterways are the Aconcagua, Mapocho, Maipo, Maule, and Bío-Bío Rivers.

The Bío-Bío River is fed by the icy waters of the Andes.

Looking at Chile's Cities

Concepción, capital of the Bío-Bío region, is in south-central Chile, on the Bío-Bío River. Originally founded in 1550 on the present site of the city of Penco, Concepción was rebuilt in its present location after being destroyed by an earthquake in 1751. Today, the city serves as a trade center for the agricultural products produced in the fertile surrounding region. Famous landmarks include the University of Concepción, Plaza de Independencia, Museo de Concepción, and the Palacio de las Tribunales. An estimated 350,268 people live in Concepción.

Viña del Mar is in central Chile on the Pacific Ocean, at the mouth of the Estero Marga-Marga River. It is contiguous with neighboring Valparaíso, so the two cities form one major metropolitan area. One of the most popular seaside resorts in Latin America, Viña del

Mar is also an important manufacturing center. It was settled by the Spaniards in 1560. Sights worth seeing include a fine arts museum and a botanical garden. The 322,220 people who live in Viña del Mar enjoy weather with an annual average daily temperature of 58°F (14°C).

Valparaíso (above), home of the National Congress, serves as a major seaport and manufacturing center. Located in central Chile on a wide bay of the Pacific Ocean, it forms a major metropolitan area with Viña del Mar. Founded in 1536, the city has been severely damaged several times by earthquakes. Santa María Technical University was established in Valparaíso in 1926, and the Catholic University of Valparaíso was founded in 1928. About 282,168 people live in the city.

The soil is rich in these river valleys. Orchards, vineyards, croplands, and pastures cover much of the territory. Chilean wine, made from grapes grown in central Chile, is famous. Mining for coal, copper, and manganese is also important in this region.

Vineyards in La Serena Valley

A waterfall in the Lakes Region

The southern part of the Central Valley is called the Lakes Region. The landscape is incredibly beautiful, filled with glacier-topped mountains, volcanic cones, waterfalls tumbling over boulders, and deep green, blue, and teal-colored lakes. Rich farmlands are interspersed among virgin forests.

Volcanoes

Chile is one of the nations in the Pacific Rim, also known as the Ring of Fire. Most of the world's volcanoes are in the regions that surround the Pacific Ocean. The Andes is a volcanic mountain range.

About fifty of Chile's volcanoes are still active. Volcanic activity has produced disasters, but it also provides some benefits to people. Steam and thermal pools created by volcanoes are a source of heat and power for industry. And in the Lakes Region, especially, volcanoes have produced a stunning landscape.

The region filled with volcanoes and lakes lies mostly south of the town of Temuco. A half-dozen national parks preserve wilderness sections of this picture-postcard area. The largest lake is Llanquihue, near the southern end of the region. Osorno Volcano, which has a perfect cone shape much like that of Japan's Mount Fuji, looms above the lake's western shore. Llanquihue is the third-largest natural lake on the South American continent. Ocean-like waves crash against its shores in rough weather.

Chile and the Pacific Ring of Fire

- Volcanoes, Ring of Fire
- Tectonic Plates

The Lakes Region is a popular tourist destination. The terrain is a paradise for mountain climbers, hikers, skiers, rafters, and other lovers of the outdoors. People come from many nations to explore the Andes and the lakes. Accommodations range from lodges and campgrounds to luxurious lakeshore hotels and ski resorts.

The lakes, fed by glacial water from the mountains, are different colors depending on how far the water has traveled. At the highest points, where the ice has just melted, the water is a milky, pale-green color. Farther on, it is a deep green that becomes more and more clear at lower elevations.

The Earthquake of 1960

"Chile is always moving and shaking," Chileans say. More than half of the nation's land is volcanic. Earthquakes, as well as volcanic eruptions, have occurred many times. During the twentieth century, more than two dozen major earthquakes shook Chile.

One of the strongest disturbances came on May 22, 1960. It was the second quake in two days. It measured 8.75 on the Richter scale, which is a measurement of the strength of earthquakes. Anything above 8.0 on this scale is considered extremely disruptive. The quake caused four volcanic eruptions and a gigantic tidal wave. The shock was felt clear across the Pacific Ocean, in Japan and New Zealand.

Fishing villages all along the coast of south-central Chile, from Puerto Saavedra to the island of Chiloé, were completely destroyed. In some areas, land dropped as much as 6 to 8 feet (1.8 to 2.4 m). The water in one lake rose 115 feet (35 m) in a single day. It took workers with heavy machinery two months to drain off the excess water and prevent permanent flooding of the San Pedro Valley.

"The crazy geography of Chile starts at Puerto Montt," a tour guide may tell a group of tourists. Puerto Montt is the main settlement in the Lakes Region. To the south, most of Chile's land consists of thousands of islands—the Archipelago. The paved *Panamericana* (Pan American Highway),

Mountain waterfalls feed a river in the Aisén Region.

which connects Chile with countries to the north, ends on the island of Chiloé. Another highway extends from Puerto Montt to Coihaique on the mainland. This winding route passes through national parks, with views of glaciers, hot springs, forests, lakes, and mountains.

The southern, narrow part of South America is in a region called Patagonia. It includes part of Argentina and the Chilean Lakes Region and the Archipelago. *Patagonia* is a Spanish word meaning "big feet." Early explorers named the region, referring to Tehuelche Indians they met who were wearing large boots.

Puerto Williams in Tierra del Fuego

The Archipelago

Cape Horn, the southernmost tip of Chile, is 1,000 miles (1,609 km) south of Puerto Montt. About 20 percent of Chile's people live in the Archipelago between these two points. In most of the region there are no railroads and only a few roads. Many of the small, widely scattered settlements are accessible only by boat. Some are on islands, and some are on stretches of mainland that are cut off from other areas by inlets, fjords, glaciers, and deep forests.

It is a wild and windswept expanse of land, ice, and water, one of the wettest and stormiest places in the world. Much of the mainland is mountainous. The mountains are not as high as those farther north, but they are incredibly steep. They rise straight up, covered with snow and glaciers. Here and there, ice fields reach right down to the ocean.

The blue color of old icebergs looks especially deep on overcast days.

Some of the glaciers are as much as a million years old. When pieces of a glacier break off and become floating icebergs, the process is called "calving." Icebergs in this region are a deep, clear blue, which indicates that they are very old and very compressed. Nearly all the oxygen has been squeezed out of them.

The Strait of Magellan separates the mainland from the *Tierra del Fuego* (Land of Fire) islands, which are divided between Chile and Argentina. The strait is a major sea-lane between the Pacific and Atlantic Oceans and a dangerous channel to navigate. However, it is a shorter route and much less hazardous than the wild, open waters around Cape Horn, south of Tierra del Fuego. Petroleum and natural gas are found in the waters of the strait. Punta Arenas, on the strait, is the Archipelago's only major settlement.

Punta Arenas, on the Strait of Magellan

The climate is a little milder and the temperatures a little warmer in Tierra del Fuego and the extreme southern end of the mainland than in the rest of the Archipelago. Some regions here have large pasturelands suitable for raising sheep.

Ferdinand Magellan

At the end of the fifteenth century, most people in the world knew almost nothing about geography. They thought the world was flat. A Portuguese explorer named Vasco da Gama had found a route from Europe to Asia around the tip of Africa. Christopher Columbus, an Italian working for Spain, had gone west, across the Atlantic Ocean to the Americas. But no one had gone all the way around the world.

Ferdinand Magellan, another Portuguese explorer, believed it would be possible to reach Asia by sailing west from Spanish America. He convinced King Charles I of Spain to finance an expedition. The goal was to find a route west, around the Americas, to the East Indies. The expedition, under Magellan's command, set out in 1519 with five ships and more than 200 men.

Magellan found a water passage at the southern tip of South America that connected the Atlantic and Pacific Oceans. He guided his three ships (two had been lost) through the connecting waterway (above). The difficult voyage through the stormy passage took thirty-eight days. The route, at the southern tip of Chile's mainland, was later named the Strait of Magellan in his honor.

Magellan is credited with leading the first expedition to sail around the world, but he did not make the entire voyage. He was killed in the Philippines in 1521. Only one ship, commanded by Juan Sebastian del Cano and carrying only seventeen crew members, made it back to Spain.

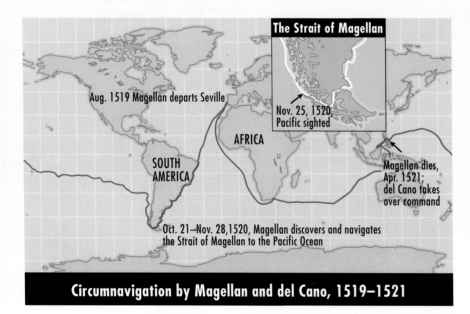

The Strait of Magellan

Aug. 1519 Magellan departs Seville

Nov. 25, 1520, Pacific sighted

AFRICA

SOUTH AMERICA

Magellan dies, Apr. 1521; del Cano takes over command

Oct. 21–Nov. 28, 1520, Magellan discovers and navigates the Strait of Magellan to the Pacific Ocean

Circumnavigation by Magellan and del Cano, 1519–1521

Chilean Antarctica

Antarctica, fifth-largest of the continents, is nearly all covered with a year-round coat of ice. Eighteen countries operate scientific stations there. The only residents are researchers connected with these stations. The Antarctic Treaty, agreed to by forty-two countries as of 1996, governs the continent. Chile claims a region that reaches to the South Pole, called *Territorio Chileno Antártica*.

Antarctica has beautiful, strange scenery and wildlife. In spite of its severe weather and the difficulty of getting there, several thousand tourists make the journey each year by ship or private yacht.

Chilean Pacific Islands

Far away in the South Pacific is a bit of Chile called Easter Island. It is also called *Isla de Pascua* in Spanish and *Rapa Nui* in Polynesian, and has been given several other names during its history. It is famous for its huge, prehistoric monoliths sculpted from volcanic stone.

Easter Island, 2,300 miles (3,700 km) from the Chilean mainland, is a small, subtropical, volcanic island. Much of it is covered with rough lava fields. There are many caves. Some of the volcanic slopes are

Prehistoric statues of Easter Island

gentle and grass-covered; some have been eroded by the ocean into almost vertical cliffs. There are no streams on this nearly barren island. Temperatures are high, moderated by frequent showers and occasional tropical rainstorms.

The Juan Fernández Islands are a bit closer to mainland Chile—a little more than 400 miles (644 km) from its coast. They are small volcanic islands, with rich vegetation, beautiful scenery, and a mild climate. Several hundred people live there, most of them in the town of San Juan Bautista. Both Easter Island and the Juan Fernández Islands are national parks.

Robinson Crusoe

Robinson Crusoe, an adventure story published in 1719, has been read by countless people around the world. Its author, Daniel Defoe, based his novel on the

experiences of a seaman named Alexander Selkirk who was marooned on a tropical island in 1704. He lived there for four years before finally being rescued by an English pirate ship. Defoe invented the details, but the island where Selkirk lived actually exists. It is one of Chile's Juan Fernández Islands.

Juan Fernández, a Portuguese adventurer who was working for the Spanish crown, first spotted these bits of land in 1574. Over the years, they became a popular stopping point for pirates. The Spanish built fortresses there in the late 1700s, and after independence, Chile took possession of the islands.

Today the largest of the three islands (left) is named Robinson Crusoe, after the popular fictional character. The second-largest is named Alexander Selkirk, for the marooned seaman, and the smallest is Santa Clara. Of the millions of people who have heard the story of Robinson Crusoe, very few have ever visited the island named for him.

Regions of Chile

The thirteen regions of Chile are numbered from north to south. They are usually referred to by their numbers, using Roman numerals. Metropolitan Santiago, which includes the capital city, is an unnumbered region.

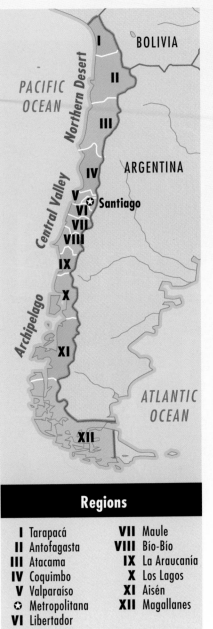

Regions

I Tarapacá	VII Maule
II Antofagasta	VIII Bío-Bío
III Atacama	IX La Araucanía
IV Coquimbo	X Los Lagos
V Valparaíso	XI Aisén
✪ Metropolitana	XII Magallanes
VI Libertador	

Region	Name	Capital	Description
I	Tarapacá	Iquique	Mostly harsh, dry desert. Port cities: Arica and Iquique.
II	Antofagasta	Antofagasta	Desert, copper mines.
III	Atacama	Copiapó	Southern part of the desert; some vegetation in valleys.
IV	Coquimbo	La Serena	Large rivers, agriculture, mining, industry, fishing.
V	Valparaíso	Valparaíso	Largest harbors in Chile; seat of Congress and Chile's second-largest city; popular resorts. Region includes Easter Island and the Juan Fernández Islands.
	Metropolitana	Santiago	Population center and hub of the nation's government, culture, education, and economy.
VI	Libertador	Rancagua	Agricultural and mining region; home of *huasos* (cowboys).
VII	Maule	Talca	Farming and forestry region.
VIII	Bío-Bío	Concepcíon	Region of hills, rivers, forests. Farming, some industry.
IX	La Araucanía	Temuco	Agriculture, herding, tourism; home of about 200,000 Araucanian Indians.
X	Los Lagos	Puerto Montt	Agriculture, forestry, tourism; beautiful terrain of lakes and volcanic mountains.
XI	Aisén	Coihaique	Harsh region of high mountains, swift rivers, fjords, glaciers. Cattle and sheep herding.
XII	Magallanes	Punta Arenas	Southernmost region, includes Chilean sections of Tierra del Fuego and Antarctica.

Living Creatures and Their Habitat

34

C HILE DOES NOT HAVE THE HUMID TROPICAL FORESTS found in some other South American countries. Because of this, species of wildlife and vegetation in Chile differ quite a lot from those on much of the rest of the continent. Chile has none of the colorful tropical birds found in such countries as Brazil. Especially in the south, the flora and fauna of Chile are more like those of New Zealand and Australia than those of the rest of South America.

Animal and plant life in Chile vary as much from one section to another as the climate and topography of the country. There are very few large land mammals anywhere. No creatures exist in Chile that present a danger to hikers or campers—no bears, no poisonous snakes. There are two kinds of poisonous spiders, but they are fairly rare.

Opposite: **Penguins coming ashore at Cape Horn**

The Huemul and the Condor

Two creatures, symbols of Chile's wildlife, appear on the national coat of arms and on Chilean coins—the huemul and the condor (right). The huemul is a rare, large, regal deer, with stiff brown hair and short legs. It is a threatened species, and the National Forestry Corporation (CONAF) is working to recover and preserve it. The condor is a large, black vulture with white neck feathers and wing patches. The largest of all birds of prey, it is spectacular to watch in flight. It has a bald head and a grand crest. A full-grown condor measures 10 feet (3 m) from wing tip to wing tip.

None of Chile's birds (some 450 species in all) migrate to North America, but some North American species come to Chile to escape northern winters. They include plovers, sandpipers, gulls, terns, osprey, peregrine falcons, and barn swallows.

In the North

The huemul, llama, alpaca, guanaco, and vicuña all live in the Andes Mountains. Mountain cats, small rodents, some insects, and lizards live among the cacti, grasses, and small trees of the north. Wild donkeys can be found in the foothills.

Lizards are common in many parts of Chile.

South American Camels

Four animals native to Chile and Peru are related to camels—the llama, the alpaca, the guanaco, and the vicuña. However, they do not have humps like camels, and their feet are narrower than camels' feet. These narrow feet make it easier for them to walk in the uneven terrain of the Andes, where they live.

Llamas and alpacas have been domesticated in South America for more than 4,000 years. Llamas can carry heavy loads and are used as pack animals (above). Alpacas are smaller than llamas and have longer, finer wool, which comes in many shades of black, brown, gray, and white. Wool from llamas and alpacas is woven, knitted, and crocheted into many articles of clothing.

Guanacos, about the same size as llamas, are wild and live in many sections of Chile, including the south. They survive in deserts, shrub lands, and savannas, and at the edge of forests. Many people believe guanacos were the original species—the ancestors of llamas, alpacas, and vicuñas.

Vicuñas are about half as large as guanacos. Both of these wild species have been hunted until they were nearly extinct. Only about 400 vicuñas survived in the wild by 1970, according to estimates. They are now protected, and their numbers have increased to more than 20,000. Guanacos and vicuñas thrive in some of Chile's national parks, especially Lauca in the north and Torres del Paine in the south.

A chinchilla

Cormorants frequent Chile's seacoast.

A few wild chinchillas are protected by the nation's Committee for Defense of Flora and Fauna. This group, with the cooperation of the University of Chile, is working to preserve this beautiful and valuable animal. The chinchilla has been exploited for its fur and inbred extensively on fur farms. Scientists are trying to save the wild creatures in order to improve the breed.

On the coast, bird life includes pelicans, penguins, and petrels. Toward the south, sea swallows and cormorants appear, and songbirds inhabit the inland regions.

Lizards are common in many parts of the country. Some are as tiny as 4 inches (10 cm), while others stretch out to more than 10 feet (3 m).

In the semi-arid desert south of Antofagasta, the only plants seen most of the time are cacti and small bushes. But once in a while there is more rain than usual, and dormant seeds and bulbs come to life. A wealth of unusual flowers appears, and insects that usually live underground emerge in search of food.

The National Flower

Chile's national flower, the copihue, is long and bell-shaped, with fleshy petals. It is usually red, but there are pink and white varieties as well. It grows on vines in the central and southern regions of the country. Chilean poet Gabriela Mistral described it this way:

> The climber betrays the grumpy austral forest; she revives it and practically makes it speak. The acrobat of the oaks and the dancer of the whitewoods harries its nursemaid-trees with the lasso of flaming fireworks.

Central Chile

Small animals, lizards, toads, and frogs live in the forests of central Chile. Mountain cats and pumas (one of the few species found throughout the Americas) prey on the smaller animals. Other forest animals include foxes, wolves, weasels, and hares.

Andean condors live in the high mountains. Three species of flamingos, hummingbirds, and a type of parrot called the Magellan conure also call the Andes home.

Beech and monkey-puzzle trees are common in the temperate forests of central Chile. The forests and grassy plains support a wide variety of vegetation. Small flocks of rheas inhabit rolling grasslands. The rhea is something like an African ostrich. Like the ostrich, it can run very fast, usually faster than its predators.

A full-grown rhea with chicks

Some alerce trees are thousands of years old.

Forests in the southern part of central Chile were cleared long ago for agriculture. Then, as the land became less productive, it eroded. In recent years, reforestation projects have begun to reclaim the land for timber. New plantings are mostly pine and eucalyptus.

A tree called the *alerce* grows in the region around Puerto Montt. It is a large, coniferous tree, somewhat similar to the California redwood. Its wood was once widely used for shingles. Some of these trees are more than 4,000 years old. Alerces have been widely overcut. Today they are considered a national treasure, and it is illegal to cut them.

Santiago Zoo

The Santiago Zoo is about the only spot in the Central Valley where one can see wildlife. This part of the country is thickly populated, and all the available open land is used for agriculture.

The zoo houses a great many animals native to Chile. Small, rare cats difficult to spot in the wild are here, as is the Chilean beaver, the *coipo.* Endangered species, such as the *pudu,* a small, reddish deer (right), are kept safe here. Visitors can see herds of all four South American camels—llamas, alpacas, guanacos, and vicuñas—and observe their differences.

A large collection of native birds includes Chilean condors, eagles, flamingos, and the unusual black-necked swans.

The South

Vegetation is sparse in the sub-Antarctic wet forest. Sphagnum moss, lichens, and bromeliads are the most common forms. Water life, on the other hand, is abundant. Steamer ducks and nine species of penguins swim near shore, along with sea leopards, sea elephants, seals, and dolphins. Farther out, in the waters between Antarctica and Chile, are huge blue whales.

An unusual small marsupial called *monito del monte* (mountain monkey) lives in the coastal mountains of southern Chile. Marsupials are animals that carry their babies in a pouch. Kangaroos and opossums are other marsupials.

Two national parks are dedicated to preserving some of Chile's precious birds. One is named for the *pinguinos* (penguins), the other for *los cisnes* (the swans).

Small herds of huemuls live in an isolated part of the southernmost high Andes. Beavers, muskrats, foxes, guanacos, pumas, and skunks are common, along with hares and other rodents.

Torres del Paine National Park

Torres del Paine is the crown jewel among Chile's national parks. Its scenery is spectacular, with towering (*torres* means "towers") snowcapped peaks, waterfalls, turquoise-colored lakes, rushing creeks and rivers, forests, and glaciers. It is a paradise for backpackers and hikers, thousands of whom arrive from around the world each year.

CONAF

Chile has about eighty protected natural areas, including national parks, forest reserves, natural monuments, and sanctuaries. Most of them are administered by the National Forestry Corporation (CONAF). These beautiful spots, many of them in the Andes, draw many visitors from other countries.

The first park, Vicente Pérez Rosales, was established in 1926. It lies between Lake Llanquihue and the border of Argentina and includes three volcanic peaks as well as the large *Lago Todos los Santos* (All Saints Lake).

Guanacos roam Torres del Paine National Park.

Not the least of the park's attractions is the abundance of wildlife. There are herds of guanacos, which allow camera-toting tourists to get quite close to them. Huemuls and pumas also live in the park, but they are not as easy to spot. Smaller animals, such as hares, foxes, and skunks, also enjoy the habitat. More than a hundred species of birds have been identified, including rheas, condors, geese, black-necked swans, ibis, parrots, and flamingos. Torres del Paine has been called a miniature Alaska.

The Pacific Islands

The Juan Fernández archipelago is a unique wilderness, with many types of animal and plant life found nowhere else in the world. For this reason, the United Nations Educational, Scientific, and Cultural Organization (UNESCO) has designated the group of islands as a World Biosphere Reserve.

CONAF workers are dedicated to preserving the flora and fauna. Among the more than a hundred categories of unusual plants are several types of giant ferns that grow as high as small trees. A unique red hummingbird with silky feathers and a needle-sharp black beak makes its home here.

The Juan Fernández seal is the only mammal native to the islands. Two centuries ago, North American sailors almost destroyed the entire population of seals in the waters around the islands. They killed millions of the water creatures for their valuable fur pelts. The wild goats, rats, rabbits, and coatis (a raccoonlike animal) were all brought in by humans. Today, the people of the islands make a living by catching fish and lobsters to sell on the mainland.

Easter Island's volcanic soil does not support much vegetation except coarse grasses and a few types of ferns. The island once had some forests, but these were cut down by the inhabitants many generations ago. Some eucalyptus trees have been planted in modern times. There is very little native animal life except for a few seabirds.

A Long and Rocky Road to Democracy

THOUSANDS OF YEARS AGO, ASIA AND THE AMERICAS were one gigantic landmass. Historians and archaeologists believe that early humans crossed a land bridge from Asia to what is now Alaska and slowly moved south. Some of them eventually reached the part of South America we now call Chile.

Not very much is known about these earliest people, but archaeologists have found clues from bones preserved in the hot, dry climate of desert areas. Some of the bones are remains of huge, prehistoric creatures that once roamed the highlands—ancestors of today's elephants, horses, and deer. Humans tracked these animals and gathered edible plants for food.

Other clues are mummies that have been found on top of Chile's high mountains. DNA tests indicate that these remains are 10,000 years old. They may be the oldest mummies in the world.

Early Life

Over thousands of years, descendants of the early settlers developed agriculture and began to live in small settlements. In the valleys, they raised livestock and grew

Opposite: **Soldiers in the wreckage of the Presidential Palace in 1973**

This mummy of a ten-year-old girl was found high in Chile's mountains.

crops such as maize and beans. People in the highlands herded alpacas and llamas. Life in coastal villages was easier. The climate was mild at sea level, and food—fish, shellfish, and sea lions—was plentiful.

Villagers built homes from adobe in some regions, stone in others, and animal skins in still others. They learned how to make baskets, pottery, and simple metal objects. They spun wool from the llamas and alpacas into yarn, dyed it with vegetable dyes, and wove it into textiles.

Local chieftains built walled fortresses in the northern desert. Trade developed between the *Atacameños* (People of the Desert) and neighboring peoples. The Tiahuanacos, from what is now Bolivia, were anxious to trade for the copper and precious stones. Llama caravans carried trade goods across the desert.

Geoglyphs and Petroglyphs

Giant murals called geoglyphs can be seen on the sides of sand dunes in several spots in Chile's northern

desert. Geometric shapes and figures of animals and people were drawn by scraping away a top layer of brown stones to expose the light sand underneath (left). An occasional arrow suggests that the pictures may have been roadside maps to guide the caravans along their trade routes. Another theory is that the figures may have had a religious significance. One drawing of a human, called *The Giant of the Atacama*, is nearly 400 feet (122 m) long.

The art of these early cultures was also expressed in petroglyphs carved into rock walls that border river valleys. Both types of ancient art date from about the eleventh to fourteenth centuries A.D., according to archaeologists.

The ancestors of these Araucanian Indians were living in Chile's Central Valley when the Incas arrived there from Peru in the fifteenth century.

In the fifteenth century, a powerful Incan society was developing in Peru, north of Chile. The Incas managed to organize many local tribes into a kind of empire. Armies, traders, and colonists spread out for long distances along the Pacific coast of South America. The Incas were skilled engineers. They built large public structures and a vast network of roads. They called the land south of their cities *Chile*, which probably meant "land's end" or "where the land runs out."

As the Incan armies moved south, they found three major native groups living in the Central Valley of Chile. Known collectively as the Araucanians, they all spoke the same language, but they had different cultures. Separately, they were called the *Picunches* (Men of the North), *Mapuches* (Men of the Land),

and *Huilliches* (Men of the South). Incan troops made their way as far south as the River Maule, which is almost halfway between Chile's northern border and the Strait of Magellan. There they met resistance from the Mapuches.

The Incan influence lasted only a few decades. Problems at home forced the troops to withdraw from the south. They left behind them a system of roads known as the Royal Road of the Incas. Travelers in northern Chile can retrace some of these routes and see remains of Incan fortresses and way stations.

An Incan way station in Chile

Arrival of the Europeans

Ferdinand Magellan, a Portuguese explorer in the service of Spain, was the first European to see the coast of Chile. In 1520, he sailed through a strait between the mainland of South America and Tierra del Fuego and proceeded north up the coast of present-day Chile. This became the strait that bears his name, but that one voyage is the only connection he made with the newly found territory.

Only a few years later, Spanish *conquistadores* (soldiers) attempted to explore Chile on horseback. Their main hope was to discover gold mines. One expedition followed a route south from Peru in 1535. They pushed forward for two years but did not find gold. Disappointment, hunger, and battles with the natives were too much for them. They returned to Peru in defeat.

Pedro de Valdivia, Conquistador

Pedro de Valdivia was born in Spain c. 1500 (c. stands for *circa*, a Latin word meaning "about"). He was a career soldier who fought in various skirmishes in Europe. In 1535, he was sent to Venezuela, then to Peru, where he was rewarded for his victories in battle. He used his reward to finance an expedition into Chile.

Valdivia had a vision for this land south of Peru. He was intrigued by the Andes Mountains, which seemed to him to be walls that sheltered Chile's fertile valleys from the rest of the world. He founded several early settlements, including Chile's present-day capital, Santiago. Valdivia was made governor of Chile in 1549 and built several more cities—Concepción, Villarrica, and the one that bears his name, Valdivia. He lost his life in a battle with the Araucanian Indians in Tucapel.

Lautaro, Mapuche Hero

Lautaro was a young man who was captured by Spanish soldiers and confined to a camp. His intelligence was obvious to his captors, and he was trained to serve as a page for Pedro de Valdivia. He was a keen observer and quickly learned a great deal about the Spanish soldiers.

After escaping from captivity, he organized a number of Mapuche leaders and taught them how to ride horseback and how to use combat tactics to fight the invaders. On Christmas Day in 1553, the Mapuches attacked the Spanish settlement of Tucapel. Valdivia was killed during this battle.

Lautaro led his people in a series of victorious battles over the next four years. They advanced north to the edge of the city of Santiago, where Lautaro was killed by a member of another native tribe. Without their leader, the Mapuches were driven back south. For the next 300 years, they managed to hold onto most of their lands in the south. Lautaro is remembered in Chilean literature as a heroic fighter for freedom.

Pedro de Valdivia was the first Spaniard to claim a spot in Chile. He founded Santiago in 1541 and set it up as a Spanish outpost. The Mapuches vigorously resisted the attempts by the foreigners to colonize their lands. The Incas had not been able to conquer the Mapuches, but the Spanish had more deadly weapons than any known by the natives. The conquistadores captured, tortured, and killed many thousands in their drive to control the land.

The Araucanians managed to hold most of the lands south of the Bío-Bío River until the 1880s. Arauco was often referred to during that period as a separate country.

The Spanish government lost interest in Chile when it seemed there was no fortune in gold there. They built a string of forts along the Bío-Bío River but pretty much ignored the land south of there. All the Spanish government wanted from Chile was to collect taxes and control trade. Chile was governed as part of the Viceroyalty of Peru. Lima was the capital.

A small, compact colonial society developed in the region between the desert and the Bío-Bío. There was a great deal of intermarriage, except among a small group of elite Spaniards at the top of the social scale. They were called *peninsulares*, meaning Spanish-born persons living in an overseas colony. Next to them in power and prestige were their Chilean-born descendants, the *criollos*. Further down the scale were *mestizos* (descendants of mixed marriages), and at the bottom, the native Indians. There were also a few slaves, who were of African descent.

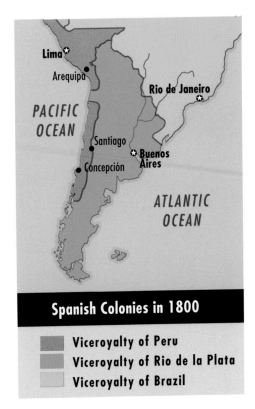

Spanish Colonies in 1800

- Viceroyalty of Peru
- Viceroyalty of Rio de la Plata
- Viceroyalty of Brazil

Representatives of the Roman Catholic Church helped strengthen Spanish control in Chile. They came to South America with the colonists. Both the Spanish governors and the missionaries believed it was their duty to convert the natives to Christianity.

The Spanish rulers set up a system of estates. Individual Spaniards, including some of the Catholic missionaries, were granted the right to control large parcels of land. The natives already living there were denied any right to the land and were forced to work for the landlords. In turn, the landholders were supposed to educate their workers in religion and the Spanish language, but this obligation was often overlooked.

The Spanish culture spread throughout the northern part of Chile during the 1600s and 1700s. As time went on, the native population dwindled. Many Indians died from exposure to new diseases and from overwork and hardship. Before long, the majority of people in Chile were mestizos.

Decline of the Spanish Empire

Spanish control over Chile was never complete. The Mapuches resisted the Spanish conquerors with the same independent spirit they had shown the Incan invaders. By the end of the eighteenth century, criollos all over South America had become more and more dissatisfied with their situation. Spanish-born aristocrats still dominated the society, and Spain controlled all the colonial trade.

Independence movements arose in many parts of the Western Hemisphere. Chileans, Venezuelans, Argentines, and Peruvians fought to drive the Spanish from the continent. British and North American merchants helped furnish weapons and ammunition to the rebels.

At first the Chileans were not thinking about national independence. They simply wanted to elect their own local governmental authorities. In 1810, they demanded the resignation of the governor appointed from Spain and chose their own authorities. At the same time, they swore allegiance to the Spanish king. They then established a National Congress. Spanish authorities repealed this early attempt at self-government and annulled all the reform actions the Congress had begun. They persecuted the leaders of the revolution. Some were exiled or imprisoned; others were shot. The harsh measures simply made the Chileans more determined to gain independence.

Bernardo O'Higgins

Bernardo O'Higgins is known as *El Libertador* (The Liberator) and the father of Chile. Born in 1778, he was the illegitimate son of Ambrosio O'Higgins, an Irish immigrant who served as colonial governor of Chile under the Spanish. In his teens, Bernardo was sent to school in London. While there he became interested in helping to overthrow Spanish control over Chile.

For several years, battles were fought between Chileans loyal to Spain and those who wanted independence. O'Higgins recruited troops and took part in a number of skirmishes. He rose to become commander-in-chief of the patriot armies in Chile. Then, in 1817, he was made supreme director—head of the first Chilean government.

O'Higgins was too conservative for the liberals and too liberal for the conservatives, however. He was forced to resign in 1823. A few years later, the government stripped him of his honors, but it restored them again before he died in 1842.

Chile's Region VI, Region Del Libertador General Bernardo O'Higgins, is named in his honor, as is a

large national park farther south, in Regions XI and XII. The park is a scenic wonderland of fjords and glaciers, populated by many sea creatures and birds.

Bernardo O'Higgins formally declared Chile's independence from Spain on February 12, 1818. At that time, Chile was a small, compact country, reaching only from the southern end of the Antofagasta region to the Bío-Bío River. In 1823, Chile abolished slavery, the first South American country to do so. The nation tried out several systems of government, under several political leaders, during the next few years.

In 1833, Chile adopted a Constitution. The Portales Constitution, named for government minister Diego Portales, lasted for nearly a century, until 1925. It provided for orderly elections, but in practice, the president and a small group of aristocrats had the real power. Only adult males who were literate and owned property were eligible to vote. Roman Catholicism was proclaimed as the official state religion. The Constitution was imperfect, but it was the first one adopted in any South American country.

The nation suffered through several short civil wars during the nineteenth century. In 1879, war broke out with the neighboring countries of Peru and Bolivia. This encounter is known as the War of the Pacific. The conflict was largely over control of the rich nitrate fields in the Atacama Desert. Chile

A sea battle during the War of the Pacific

was victorious, but over the next few decades the country's nitrate industry became controlled by investors in Britain and the United States.

Nitrate and copper mining brought prosperity to Chile—at least to some of the people. Antofagasta and Iquique became important international ports because of nitrate exports.

Meanwhile, large landowners continued to dominate Chilean society. Over time, the country expanded north and south to its present borders. The development of railroads, military battles with neighboring countries, and treaties with the Mapuches made the expansion possible.

The economy of Chile was changing. A middle class of factory owners and merchants developed. They began to resent the fact that power was concentrated in the presidency and a few large landholders. They wanted to elect a Congress that could represent their interests.

A civil war broke out in 1891. Thousands of people were killed. Supporters of a more powerful Congress gained some ground, but more strife was to come. Miners and other workers were beginning to organize into mutual aid societies and leftist political parties. They held protest meetings and resorted to strikes.

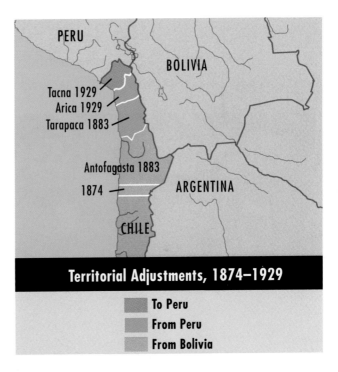

Territorial Adjustments, 1874–1929

To Peru
From Peru
From Bolivia

Several violent encounters erupted between miners and agents of the mine owners. One of these conflicts was especially bloody. In 1907 the army was called in to break up a strike meeting in Iquique. The peaceful meeting was suddenly turned into a massacre. Hundreds of men, women, and children were slaughtered by machine-gun fire.

The Twentieth Century

A new Constitution was written in 1925. There were many important changes. The Constitution provided for separation of church and state, recognized the right of workers to organize labor unions, and promised to provide for the welfare of all citizens. It spelled out the powers of four branches of government: executive, legislative, judicial, and comptroller general.

Salvador Allende

The Chilean people began to take an increased interest in politics. Many political parties developed, representing opinions that ranged from the far left to the far right. The extreme points of view made it difficult to find areas of agreement, but an uneasy balance prevailed for several decades.

Salvador Allende Gossens, a socialist, was elected president in 1970. He quickly attempted to reform various industries, such as banking, insurance, and communications. He succeeded in nationalizing the copper industry. Right-wing and moderate elements, feeling threatened by these reforms and fearful of losing their privileges, were determined to destroy the Allende government. They turned to a military leader, General Augusto Pinochet, to oust the president.

In 1973, troops entered Santiago in tanks and seized the government. It was a *coup d'état* (a French term meaning "overthrow of a government"). Among the thousand or so

The Presidential Palace burning after it was bombed during the military takeover in 1973

people who lost their lives during the coup was President Allende, who remained in the presidential offices while they were bombed by the Chilean Air Force. Most official sources report that he committed suicide, but his supporters believed he was murdered. Scholars are still debating this controversy.

General Pinochet was the undisputed head of the military government. He dissolved the National Congress and banned all political parties. He also took control of local governments.

In 1974, Pinochet was declared president of Chile. To make the regime look legitimate, he directed a commission to draft a new Constitution. He claimed he wanted to see an orderly transition to a truly democratic government, and he directed the commission to write a Constitution that would make this possible.

The Constitution of 1980 was passed, supposedly by a national vote by the people. But the vote was totally under the control of the existing government, and the outcome was fixed. The Constitution made Pinochet president until 1989 and provided for a national vote in 1988 to keep the general in power for another eight years.

Pinochet's regime was harsh and cruel. Congress did not meet during the transition period, and all forms of opposition were swiftly suppressed. Political parties, labor organizations, freedom

Thousands of people who opposed General Pinochet's military government were rounded up and held prisoner.

of speech—all civil rights were denied. Thousands of people were openly killed or declared missing. Their families never knew what happened to them. Even today, these victims are called "The Disappeared."

Pinochet's economic measures did not restore the nation to prosperity. There was widespread unemployment, foreign debt grew enormously, and the economy lost ground. Opposition to the dictatorship grew.

A plebiscite—a direct vote by the people—was held in 1988, as the Constitution provided. Pinochet's name was the only one on the presidential ballot. However, much to the surprise of the officials, the people of Chile had organized a movement to simply vote "no" instead of voting for Pinochet. The outcome was 54.5 percent opposed to Pinochet.

President Patricio Aylwin Azócar

Patricio Aylwin Azócar was chosen president in a peaceful democratic election on December 14, 1989. It was the first democratic election since the coup. He took office in 1990. A member of the Christian Democratic Party, he also headed a coalition that included several other parties. Once again, Chile was on a road to a more representative democratic government.

Aylwin was succeeded in 1994 by Eduardo Frei Ruiz-Tagle, the son of a former president, who was elected to serve a six-year term. In the 1999 presidential election, no candidate received a majority of votes. Socialist Ricardo Lagos won the January 2000 runoff election.

A Government in Transition

C HILE IS A REPRESENTATIVE DEMOCRACY, ONE OF THE oldest in the Americas. The government of the Republic of Chile has developed out of many Western traditions. Its founders used the Constitution of the United States as an example in writing their own document. The system of courts is a mixture of Roman law, the Napoleonic Code, and Spanish traditions. The National Congress was established in 1811.

Opposite: **The Senate in session**

Chile's first national Constitution, also the first in all of South America, was enacted in 1833. Called the Portales Constitution, it was in effect for ninety-two years. Its most important provisions were the separation of governmental powers, regular elections, and a system of transferring authority from one government to the next in an orderly fashion. A new Constitution written in 1925 lasted until the military coup of 1973 and the Pinochet dictatorship that followed.

Salvador Allende Gossens

Salvador Allende Gossens, born in 1908, was brought up in an upper-middle-class family. He became interested in Marxist politics while in school. He earned a medical degree but was drawn to politics more than medicine. After finishing medical school, he helped to found the Socialist Party of Chile. He held several government offices and ran three times, unsuccessfully, for the presidency.

On his fourth try, in 1970, Allende was elected by a coalition called the Popular Unity Front. As president, he nationalized (placed under government control) the copper industry and took over large estates in a land-reform program. These measures were popular at first, and the people at the bottom of the economic scale were better off. Soon, however, the economy started a downward slide. The government didn't have the money to carry out the reforms Allende wanted to put in place. Inflation skyrocketed.

Right-wing and moderate parties formed a coalition to bring down Allende. In September 1973, the army seized control of the government by military force. It was reported that Allende committed suicide, although his supporters refused to believe this.

General Augusto Pinochet Ugarte

Born in 1915, Augusto Pinochet Ugarte attended a military academy in his teens and became a career army man. He led the army troops that seized control of Chile's government in 1973. General Pinochet was made president of the military government in 1974 and was elected president in 1981 under a new Constitution. His economic policies were conservative. He was defeated in a presidential election in 1988, but he retained his position as head of the Chilean army. A special provision of the Constitution gave him the right to hold the office of senator for the rest of his life.

Pinochet's story is unfinished. Under his regime, there were widespread violations of human rights. Thousands of people were tortured or killed, and thousands more just disappeared. People in many parts of the world felt the general should be punished for crimes against humanity.

In 1998, Pinochet went to London for back surgery. He was eighty-three years old. The government of Spain issued a warrant for his arrest for crimes against humanity. British law enforcers honored the warrant and put him under house arrest. Later, the British announced they would begin proceedings to extradite him to Spain.

Many Chileans were upset about this. The general still had many supporters at home, and even people who wanted him tried and punished thought this should happen in Chile, not in a foreign country. There were riots in Santiago and demonstrations in London.

The controversy over Pinochet's arrest created a difficult problem in international relations. Some nations were reluctant to jeopardize their good relations with the Chilean government. Some government leaders in other countries feared a trial in Spain might set a precedent that could be used in the future against other heads of government.

A third Constitution was imposed on the people by the military government in 1980. It included many good provisions that eventually helped the people develop a more democratic society. But the country continued to be governed by a military dictatorship for several more years.

After Pinochet's defeat in the 1988 plebiscite, leaders of the government and the opposition representing many points of view met to decide on necessary amendments to the Constitution. They agreed on fifty-four changes, and the recommendations were submitted to the people for a vote. The changes were approved by a huge majority—85.7 percent.

Today, the national government consists of three branches—executive, legislative, and judicial—plus several autonomous agencies. These agencies, which are not directly controlled by any of the other branches, are the Comptroller General, Constitutional Tribunal, National Security Council, Central Bank Council, Production Development Corporation, National Women's Service, and National Energy Commission.

The executive and legislative branches are separated physically, as well as legally, in Chile. The city of Santiago is the national capital, where the president resides. Since 1990, the National Congress has been located two hours away from Santiago, in the city of Valparaíso.

The Presidential Palace in Santiago

Executive Branch

Chile's president is the chief administrator of the government. The president is elected by direct popular vote and must receive a

Santiago: Did You Know This?

Santiago is located on the Mapocho River in the central part of Chile, at an altitude of 1,700 feet (518 m). Founded in 1541, it is the nation's capital as well as its largest city and principal cultural, manufacturing, transportation, and commercial center. The city is home to the Presidential Palace, the National Library, the Stock Exchange, and numerous museums.

More than 4 million people live in Santiago. In January, the average temperature ranges from 53°F to 85°F (12°C to 29°C), and in July, from 37°F to 59°F (3°C to 15°C). The average annual rainfall in the capital is 14 inches (36 cm).

Santiago

majority of votes to win. If there are more than two candidates and no one has a majority, as in 1999, a second election is held to choose between the top two. The winner serves for a six-year term and is not permitted to run for a second consecutive term. He or she must be a citizen, born in Chile, and at least forty years of age.

The president oversees the administration of the government and appoints members of the cabinet, ambassadors, and regional administrators. These appointments do not require consent of the Senate. Various other government officeholders are appointed by the president with the Senate's consent. The president also conducts international relations and serves as commander-in-chief of the armed forces.

Legislative Branch

The Chilean National Congress consists of two legislative houses—the Senate and the Chamber of Deputies. Candidates for either house must have completed a secondary

CHILE'S NATIONAL GOVERNMENT

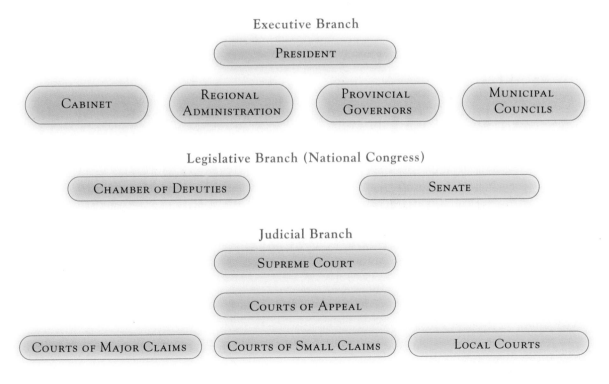

Executive Branch

PRESIDENT

CABINET   REGIONAL ADMINISTRATION   PROVINCIAL GOVERNORS   MUNICIPAL COUNCILS

Legislative Branch (National Congress)

CHAMBER OF DEPUTIES   SENATE

Judicial Branch

SUPREME COURT

COURTS OF APPEAL

COURTS OF MAJOR CLAIMS   COURTS OF SMALL CLAIMS   LOCAL COURTS (high school) education and have lived for two years in the district they represent. Senators must be at least forty years old, deputies at least twenty-one.

The 120 deputies are elected by popular vote, 2 from each of 60 electoral districts. All deputies serve for four-year terms. Every four years, new elections are held for all 120 seats.

The National Congress building in Valparaíso

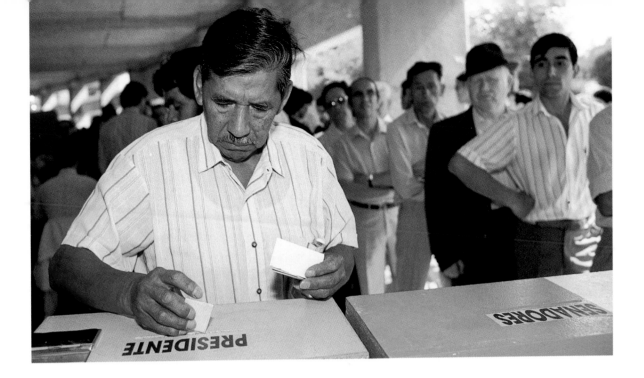

Voting on election day

Voters elect thirty-eight senators, two from each of nineteen senatorial districts. Nine additional senators are named by different branches of government. All serve eight-year terms without possibility of reelection. Elections are held every four years, with half the districts voting each time. A special provision was written into the Constitution in order to preserve General Pinochet's influence over the government. Former presidents, if they have served for at least six years, are called senators for life.

The Congress has the primary responsibility for proposing laws and constitutional reforms, but the president also has a great deal of power in the legislative area.

Judicial Branch

The Supreme Court of Chile has seventeen members. They are selected by the president from a list of candidates suggested by

Flag and Coat of Arms

Chile's national flag is divided into three sections. The bottom half is red, standing for the blood of the nation's

heroes. The top half is divided into a blue square on the left and a white rectangle on the right. A five-pointed white star, standing for progress and honor, is in the center of the blue square, which symbolizes the sky. The white rectangle is for the snow of the Andes.

Chile's official coat of arms has a shield in the center, with a five-pointed silver star against a blue-and-red background. It is topped by a plume of red, white, and blue feathers. Two native Andean creatures, a condor and a huemul, hold the shield on each side. A ribbon below bears the motto *Por la Razón o la Fuerza* (By Reason or by Force).

the court itself. Judges and prosecutors for the sixteen Courts of Appeals are appointed in the same manner. Court cases are first brought before regular courts or special courts for matters involving juveniles, labor, police, or the military.

Autonomous Agencies

The Office of the Comptroller General is the nation's auditor and oversees expenditures of funds. This office also reviews laws and resolutions before they are passed to make sure they are constitutional.

The Constitutional Tribunal has the last word on constitutional questions. In the United States, Congress passes laws that are then tested in the courts. In Chile, the tribunal acts before the fact. It can prevent laws that it rules unconstitutional from being passed.

The National Security Council advises the president on matters concerned with security. The Central Bank Council safeguards the stability of Chilean currency. The three other autonomous agencies are the Production Development Corporation, the National Women's Service, and the National Energy Commission.

Local Government

Chile is divided into thirteen regions. Regional administrators are appointed by the president. Regional councils are made up of government employees. Regional administration is managed by the national government.

Since 1992, for the first time in Chile's history, municipal officers have been elected by the people. They have autonomous control over local finances and resources. This is an important step toward putting more power in the hands of democratically elected leaders.

Eduardo Frei Ruiz-Tagle

President Eduardo Frei Ruiz-Tagle was born in Santiago in 1942. His father, Eduardo Frei Montalva, served as Chile's president from 1964 to 1970. The son, a member of the Christian Democratic Party, worked in his father's presidential campaign while still studying at the university.

The older Frei died in 1982, and his son worked hard in the campaign to vote "no" in the Pinochet plebiscite in 1988. The following year he was elected senator by a huge majority. On December 11, 1993, Frei was elected for a six-year term to succeed President Patricio Aylwin.

Presidents Aylwin and Frei both worked to restore civil rights to the Chilean people and to promote good international relations.

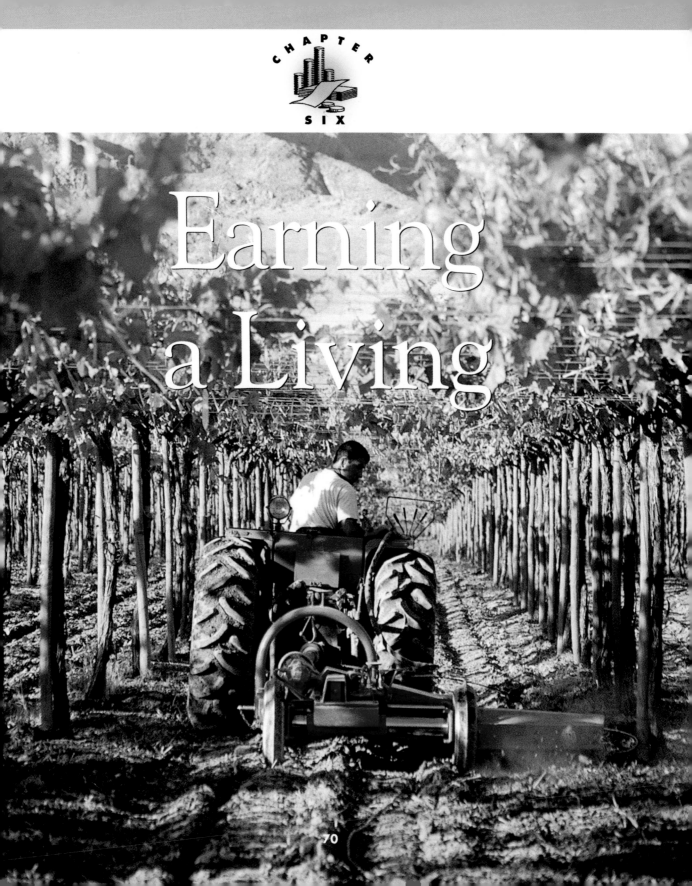

Earning a Living

THE FIRST SPANISH SETTLERS CAME TO SOUTH AMERICA with high hopes of getting rich. Privileged noblemen were granted large tracts of land, on which they developed *haciendas* (plantations). Each hacienda was a self-sufficient community, producing food, clothing, and handcrafted goods for local needs, as well as some items for trade. Most of the good agricultural land was gradually absorbed into the haciendas, and small farmers and tenants became dependent on the Spanish-born landowners for employment and livelihood.

Opposite: **Working in a vineyard**

Farming, Forestry, and Fishing

The hacienda system dominated agriculture and rural life in Chile from early colonial times until late in the twentieth century. Today, smaller farms and orchards produce abundant crops. Apples, grapes, pears, lemons, and peaches are grown

Peaches are grown for export to other countries.

Packing grapes for shipment

Sheep ranching is an important industry in the south.

for export. They are prepared for shipment in huge fruit-packing plants. Other leading farm products are beans, cattle, peas, flaxseed, hemp, and sunflowers. Recent improvements in agricultural methods have increased production of wheat, corn, and potatoes.

Wine was important to the Spanish settlers, both as a part of their diet and for use as a sacrament in religious services. The Spanish found that the soil and climate of Chile were ideal for growing grapes and making wine. The Chilean wine industry began with the first settlers. This country's wines are now famous around the world. Only France and Italy sell more wines to the United States than Chile does.

The Chilean government has a program of planting trees on lands that were once used for farming. Much of this was originally forest that had been cleared for agriculture long ago. The soil was of poor quality for crops, and reforestation has helped expand the manufacture of wood products.

In the south, on both sides of the Strait of Magellan, the major industry is sheep ranching. Huge ranches were established late in the nineteenth century by immigrants from Europe, and several families became very rich and powerful. Land reforms in 1960 broke up the large estates. The properties were distributed among settlers and workers, who continued to raise sheep on smaller farms.

Chile's fishing industry has expanded rapidly in recent years. The nation's waters are exceptionally pure and high in oxygen content. Fish flourish in these conditions— more than a thousand species are found in Chilean waters. Fish and marine products are exported all over the world. Chilean salmon, grown in fish farms, is in great demand. This country ranks second in the world in exports of salmon, after Norway. About one of every five workers in Chile is employed in farming, fishing, or forestry.

Fishing boats in a harbor on Chiloé Island

A salmon farm

production of Chilean copper. Copper soon replaced nitrates as Chile's major export, and it remains so today.

By 1918, U.S. investors controlled nearly 90 percent of the industry. Under President Allende, the government took over control of the copper industry in Chile in 1971. The new national copper corporation, CODELCO, became the largest mining and refining company in the world. Copper accounted for more than 40 percent of the nation's total exports. In spite of the importance of mining, the copper industry employs fewer than 3 percent of Chile's workforce, and it represents less than 7 percent of the nation's total production of goods and services.

Oil and gas were discovered on both sides of the Strait of Magellan, as well as offshore, in 1945. The petroleum industry is now the most important part of the economy in Tierra del Fuego.

An oil-drilling platform in the Strait of Magellan

The World's Largest Open-Pit Mine

The statistics describing the Chuquicamata copper mine are staggering. Just imagine a hole in the ground 2 1/2 miles (4 km) long, 1 1/4 miles (2 km) wide, and nearly 2,100 feet (640 m) deep! Some 9,000 workers process 60,000 tons of copper a day from this mine, the largest open-pit mine in the world. The gigantic trucks that carry the ore have tires more than 11 feet (3.4 m) in diameter. The Chuquicamata mine, now controlled by the Chilean government, produces about half the nation's total copper output. People who travel to this remote spot in the desert can take a guided tour of the mine, conducted in Spanish or English.

Manufacturing

One out of six persons in Chile's workforce is employed in manufacturing. Textiles and clothing, machinery, transportation equipment, and industrial chemicals are among the leading manufactured products. Others include processed foods, furniture and appliances, recreational boats, books and magazines, shoes, and toys.

Labor

Miners in Chile's northern labor camps at the beginning of the twentieth century were not happy with their situation.

They were paid very little and received their payment in tokens that they could use only at the company stores. This made them almost slaves of the mine owners. They began to band together, first in mutual aid societies, then in unions. The only weapons they had were protest marches and strikes, but the mine owners fought back with violence.

One incident in 1907 was particularly brutal. About 6,000 people—miners and their families—were assembled at a strike rally in Iquique. The owners called in army troops, who shot and killed about 30 members of the strike committee standing on a balcony. They then turned their guns on the audience. Hundreds of men, women, and children were massacred.

Membership in unions had ups and downs during the twentieth century. The Constitution of 1925 legalized workers' right to organize, but several laws were passed that restricted bargaining and imposed strict governmental controls over unions.

Soon after the military coup of 1973, all activities by unions and political parties were banned. A Labor Plan enacted in 1979 placed additional controls on collective bargaining and strikes. A decade later, with the election of President Aylwin and the transition to democracy, membership in unions began to grow rapidly.

Legislation enacted since 1989 has established many safeguards for working people. Workers' rights include a minimum wage, overtime pay, paid holidays and vacations, maternity leave, on-the-job accident insurance, the right to join a union, and regulations to safeguard health and safety.

The Future

The Chilean government is committed to encouraging an economy based on private enterprise and free trade. The economy expanded rapidly between 1989 and 1998. The volume of exports increased, and unemployment decreased. What the future brings will depend to a large extent on world markets. Chile's destiny is linked with the financial stability of nations all around the world.

Chilean Currency

The monetary unit of Chile is the *peso*, which was introduced in 1975 to replace the *escudo*. 100 *centavos* (cents) equal 1 peso. Paper bills exist in notes of 500, 1,000, 2,000, 5,000, and 10,000 pesos. Coins are available in denominations of 1, 5, 10, 50, and 100 pesos. The peso is represented with the symbol "$" or "CLP."

Chilean bills honor historic national figures. The 10,000-peso note has a picture of Don Arturo Prat Chicon on the face. Prat, the captain of a frigate, was a naval hero during the War of the Pacific. The reverse side of the bill has a picture of his birthplace in Ninhue (right), which is now a national monument.

Gabriela Mistral, Chile's Nobel Prize–winning poet, is on the face of the 5,000-peso note. To her left, a statue of a woman and two children symbolizes the poet's deep love and sympathy for children.

Muses of the arts are on the reverse, one with a harp, another writing on a manuscript.

Ignacio Carrera Pinto, another hero of the War of the Pacific, is the figure on the 1,000-peso note. The Carrera family (Ignacio's grandfather and two uncles) were prominent in the struggle for Chile's independence. The reverse of this bill pictures a monument to all Chilean heroes.

Chilean coins are imprinted with the national coat of arms, a shield held by a bird (the condor) and a deer (the huemul).

Los Chilenos

M ost Chileans are of mixed Spanish and native South American ancestry. They speak Spanish with a Chilean accent and consider themselves Roman Catholics. They live in central Chile, in a town or city of more than 20,000 people. They have dark hair and brown eyes. This general description does not fit everybody, of course, but about two-thirds of the people in the nation have these characteristics.

Opposite: **A young man from Torres del Paine National Park**

A young woman in Santiago

Who Lives in Chile?

95% are of mixed European—mostly Spanish—and native ancestry.

3% are native South Americans.

2% have other ethnic backgrounds.

77% live in central Chile, between Copiapó and Concepción.

77% are Roman Catholic.

85% live in urban areas.

About 28% are under age 15.

In spite of the great distance between the northern and southern boundaries of this long and narrow country, Chileans regard themselves as quite homogeneous, or similar. Chilean Spanish is spoken with a slightly different accent from Spanish in other Latin American countries, but it is very much the same all over Chile. Radio and television have made this even more true today than it used to be.

The Native People

The Spaniards who first came to Chile encountered many tribes of people living there. The natives did not give up their lands easily. Battles between the conquistadors and native South Americans went on for 300 years. Most of the tribes no longer exist. Many people were tortured and killed; others died of disease or starvation. Still others were absorbed into the Spanish culture through intermarriage.

More than nine out of ten Chileans today are *mestizos* (of mixed ancestry). The Spanish heritage is prominent because Spain kept sending more and more soldiers to defend their

colony. So the number of Spaniards grew as the native population was dying out.

The Mapuches (or Araucanians) who lived in south-central Chile were the strongest resisters to Spanish control. *Mapuches* means "men of the land," and they were determined to hold onto theirs. They had resisted domination by the Incas before the Spaniards came.

Most Chileans today are mestizos.

A Mapuche man

Mapuches continued to occupy their own independent territory for many years during the colonial period. Some historians have called the Mapuches fierce and militaristic. However, early missionaries described them as peaceful and friendly.

Since the 1880s, many Mapuches have lived on *reducciónes* (reservations) in south-central Chile. They are very poor, but they continue to speak their own language and defend their culture and customs. Estimates of the total number of Mapuches in Chile vary widely. Some sources say there are as few as 250,000; others, as many as 1 million.

Another, smaller group of natives lives in the mountains of northern Chile. These are the Aymarás, who number between 15,000 and 20,000. A few other natives, the Huilliches, descendants of seafaring nomads, live in scattered small villages in the archipelago.

An Aymará herder with a llama

Natives of Easter Island

The 2,000 Rapa Nui, natives of Easter Island, have an entirely different heritage. Their origin is one of the great mysteries of the world. These people live almost 1,200 miles (1,931 km) from any other inhabited place and have no written history prior to the Spanish invasion of their island. There is evidence of long-ago migrations to Easter Island from both the east (South America) and the west (Polynesia), but where the first Easter Islanders came from is not known.

Easter Island Mysteries

Where the people of Easter Island originally came from is only one of the mysteries of this strange, tiny, far-away volcanic island. Some years ago the Norwegian explorer Thor Heyerdahl published a book called *Aku-Aku*. (The title means "sleeping ghosts" in Rapa Nui, the language of Easter Island.) Heyerdahl had a theory that the first Easter Islanders came from South America. Most archaeologists, however, still believe they originated in the Polynesian islands.

How did they get to Easter Island? What is the meaning of the strange writing (below), called *rongo-rongo*, that has been found on wooden boards on the island? Why were the natives of this island the only people in all of Polynesia and the Americas who developed a written script? And above all, what is the story behind the several hundred remarkable statues of human forms that were carved here centuries ago?

Many of the *moais*, as the statues (above) are called, are as much as 30 feet (9 m) tall. Originally they were mounted on large stone platforms called *ahu*. How did the primitive people, who left behind no other evidence of advanced engineering knowledge, manage to create these giants? How did they move them from the quarry where the cutting started? How did they hoist them onto the platforms? And were they idols, or what other purpose did they have?

Early European visitors—the first ones we know of arrived in 1722—reported seeing the statues erect on the platforms. Years later they were all lying on the ground, some of them broken. How and why did this happen?

Without a written history, no one can give definite answers to any of these questions. But the statues—some of which have been restored and returned to their original standing position—serve a purpose today. They draw tourists to Easter Island, and this brings some income to the few residents. Fortunately, the antiquities have some protection from damage because Easter Island is now a national park.

Population distribution in Chile

The government is working to assist the native peoples to climb out of poverty, but they are still underprivileged. Some of them who move to the cities to find a better life adopt Spanish surnames. They hope this will help them fit into Spanish society.

Government policy, under the Law for Indigenous Peoples, recognizes the right of native peoples to live according to their own traditions. It allows each community to maintain its own culture and language and provides for intercultural and bilingual education.

Immigration

Slavery was not important to the Chilean economy. Spanish settlers didn't need large numbers of workers to manage their lands. In fact, slavery was abolished in Chile in 1823, much earlier than in most of the Americas. For this reason, unlike most other Latin American countries, Chile has never had many Africans.

Many of the settlers who came to Chile during the eighteenth century were Basques—people who lived in the Pyrenees Mountains on the border between Spain and France. After Chile became an independent country, the government decided to welcome immigration from other European countries besides Spain. This policy succeeded in attracting quite a

Chilean Names

Chileans normally use two family names—first, the father's name, and then the mother's. In some cases, the mother's two names are kept, hyphenated. In everyday use, however, the mother's family name is dropped. For example, President Eduardo Frei Ruiz-Tagle is generally referred to as President Frei.

When a woman marries, she usually substitutes her husband's family name for her mother's, but she is still generally known by her father's name, as she was before marriage. When Marta Larraechea Bolivar married Eduardo Frei Ruiz-Tagle, she became Marta Larraechea de Frei.

few German and Swiss settlers, beginning in the 1840s. The newcomers settled primarily in and near Valdivia. French and Italian farmers followed.

A woman from the German community in Valdivia

The European immigrants were absorbed into the influential upper layers of society, along with the Spanish. They brought a variety of skills with them and established businesses and factories.

In Valdivia, they erected buildings that reflected the German style of architecture. Many of the original buildings were destroyed in the 1960 earthquake, but the German influence is still evident. Streets have German names and German food is popular there. There are German schools, and about half of the people in the area speak German as well as Spanish. German farmers founded Puerto Montt in the 1850s. By 1860, there were 30,000 German immigrants in Chile.

In the 1860s, sheep farmers from England established large sheep ranches in the Magallanes

Chilean Language

Spanish is Chile's official language. Chileans speak *castellano*—Castilian Spanish—but without the lisp that is characteristic of some Spanish-speaking areas. Their pronunciation is crisp and fast, with the final syllables shortened or cut off. Consonants are sometimes slurred over. The Chilean accent is quite similar throughout the length of Chile. However, other Latin Americans sometimes have difficulty understanding the Chilean pronunciation.

A few native languages are still in use, but most native-language speakers also speak Spanish. Some of the native people in northern Chile speak Aymará, and a half-million or more Mapuches use their native tongue. Many words spoken by Chileans are taken from Mapuche.

As you read about Chile, it is helpful to know the meanings of a few Spanish words. Try pronouncing them. Just memorize how the vowels sound in Spanish. They are always pronounced the same way:

a	sounds like *a* in *father*
e	sounds like *ay* as in *date*
i	sounds like *ee* as in *feed*
o	sounds like *oh* as in *no*
u	sounds like *oo* as in *boot*

Here are a few words to practice on:

altiplano	high plain
caliente	hot
cueca	Chile's national dance
fria	cold
mestizo	of mixed descent
pampa	plain
peninsulares	Spanish-born settlers in Chile
tierra	land
torres	towers

Region, both on the mainland and on Tierra del Fuego. A gold rush in 1883 brought more Europeans, mainly Serbs and Croatians, to Tierra del Fuego.

Over the next few decades, more Spaniards, as well as Italians, East European Jews, Lebanese, Palestinians, and Syrians, established new homes in Chile. The immigrant population was still comparatively small, less than 10 percent of the total.

Urbanization

Most of today's Chileans live in urban areas. The population density varies tremendously from one part of the country to

another. There are more than 400 times as many people per square mile in the Santiago Metropolitan Region as there are in parts of the archipelago.

The movement from countryside to cities has been especially rapid since the 1960s. Rapid growth of cities brings many problems, such as traffic jams, air and water pollution, and increased crime. There has not been enough affordable housing to take care of the newcomers. An estimated 5 million people live in a ring of shantytowns called *poblaciones* or *callampas* (mushrooms), around the edge of Santiago. Most of these areas have city services, such as electricity, running water, sewer connections, and garbage collection, but many of the streets are not paved. There are fewer stores in the shantytowns, and those that exist are apt to have fewer items for sale and charge higher prices than stores in other areas.

A shantytown in Santiago

Population of Major Cities (1995 est.)

Santiago	4,295,593
Concepción	350,268
Viña del Mar	322,220
Valparaíso	282,168

Beliefs and Celebrations

IT HAS OFTEN BEEN SAID THAT THE SPANISH CAME TO THE New World with a cross and a sword. The *conquistadores* (soldiers) came prepared to take over the land, and missionaries came with them to convert the native peoples to Christianity. Both succeeded in their missions.

For several centuries, nearly all Chileans were practicing Roman Catholics. But the native South Americans had their own beliefs, and they did not give them up easily, or entirely. For the most part, they simply added the teachings of the Catholic Church to what they already believed in.

Opposite: **Santo Domingo Church in La Serana**

A church in the Atacama Region

Native Beliefs

Mapuche religion is based on belief in a natural balance between positive and negative forces—good and evil. One god represents creation and love; another is the god of illness, sin, death, and destruction. The Spanish arrival upset the natural balance, threatening destruction to the Mapuche way of life. It was important to fight this evil influence.

Women, according to Mapuche belief, can communicate directly with the gods. Religious rituals are accompanied by musical rituals, using percussion and wind instruments.

On the island of Chiloé, good and evil are personified in the legends of Pincoya and Trauco. Pincoya is an ocean goddess who dances on the waves or sunbathes on rocks. She is the goddess of fertility. If she is facing the ocean, there will be an abundance of fish. If she is facing inland, the fishers will have no luck. Pincoya's counterpart is an ugly, mean dwarf. He lives in the forest and amuses himself by attacking men and seducing women. In the mountain regions, tradition says that gods live in the volcanoes.

Spanish Missionaries

Members of the *Compaña de Jesús* (the Jesuits) were the first Catholic missionaries in Chile. They did much more than preach their religion—they educated the native people as well. They taught such skills as farming and carpentry. They also promoted European values and customs, often at the expense of the natives' own culture. Over the years, the Jesuit landholdings prospered and many of the church fathers

Fray Jorge

A forest near La Serena is named *Fray* (Brother) Jorge, after an English sailor who arrived in Chile in 1627. His vessel had been shipwrecked, and he was rescued by a Spanish ship and taken ashore. Greatly frightened by the huge storm that had caused the wreck, he had made a vow to God. He swore he would join the first Catholic religious order he could find. This turned out to be the Monastery of San Francisco.

Fray Jorge was a model of humility and devotion during his years at the monastery. He helped with all the work, which included construction of the church. The brothers were having trouble finishing the roof because they could not find enough wood. In a dream, Fray Jorge was told to take a cart and follow the oxen. He did so, and was led to a forest where he gathered a cartload of timber. The name of the forest commemorates this story.

became quite rich and powerful. Another group of Catholic missionaries, the Franciscans, also helped convert the native Chileans to Christianity.

Many of the church fathers were closely allied to the top layer of Spanish colonial society. As such, they were loyal to the king of Spain. As the independence movement gained ground in Chile, its leaders became increasingly distrustful of the Church. Nevertheless, when the Constitution of 1833 became the law of the new nation, Roman Catholicism was named the official state religion. Public practice of any other religion was forbidden. The church was in total control of education, marriages, and many other aspects of Chilean society.

Later on in the nineteenth century, English and German immigrants arrived in the nation. Most of them were Protestants, and they insisted on freedom to practice their own faith.

This man helped build this German-style church near Puerto Montt.

Religions of Chile*

Roman Catholic	77%
Protestant	13%
Atheist or agnostic	7%
Other (including Jewish and Muslim)	4%

*Does not equal 100% due to rounding.

They began to found their own schools and send their own missionaries to the native Chileans.

Religion in Chile Today

The Chilean Constitution of 1925 provided for separation of church and state. People were now free to practice other faiths. This was a benefit to international trade, because Muslims and Jews, as well as Protestants, were among the businesspeople who came to Chile from other lands.

Catholicism continued to be the dominant religion in Chile. For the first half of the twentieth century, the Catholic leaders were almost all aristocrats and politically conservative. In the 1930s, some activists began to be very interested in the progressive social doctrines of the Roman Catholic Church. These reformers united with other political groups to form the Christian Democratic Party.

During the military regime of General Pinochet (1974–1990), Catholics and Protestants worked together in support of human rights and social justice. Priests were active in the resistance, at great risk to themselves.

Protestant churches, mostly the Pentecostal and Evangelical denominations, have been gaining membership in Chile in recent years. Among the poorer people in cities, there are about as many practicing Protestants as Catholics.

On the whole, however, Chile is still overwhelmingly a Catholic nation. The 1992 census reported that almost 77 percent of the nation's population declared themselves Catholic, and only about 13 percent were Protestant. The

Roadside Shrines

At many spots along the highways in Chile, travelers see small shrines. Some are carved into a niche in a rock or hillside; others are created from small piles of stones. An arrangement includes a cross, some candles and flowers, and perhaps a photograph or two.

These little altars usually mark the spot where one or more persons died in an accident or met another type of violent death. They represent a mixture of Catholic and other beliefs. Those who erect the shrines may be devout Catholics who come to pray for the soul of a person who died without benefit of last rites. Or they may be practicing a traditional belief and trying to appease angry spirits who haunt the scene of the tragedy.

proportion of Protestants had more than doubled, however, in only 22 years. About 7 percent of the people stated they had no religion, and the remaining 4 percent were of Jewish, Muslim, Christian Orthodox, and other faiths.

The Catholic influence is reflected in the fact that Chile is one of the few remaining nations of the world where divorce is illegal. However, it is possible for couples to obtain a legal separation or an annulment of their civil marriage. Abortions are illegal, but a rapidly declining birthrate is evidence that birth-control methods are widely used.

This church in Chiu-Chiu is one of the oldest churches in Chile.

Conversion of the native South Americans to Catholicism started in the desert region of Antofagasta. Many picturesque churches in the altiplano are hundreds of years old and have been declared national monuments by the Chilean government. Some of the best examples are in the villages of Parinacota, Isluga, and Matilla.

Pedro de Valdivia's first settlement was Chiu-Chiu, on the Inca road from Peru through Chile. Chiu-Chiu's Iglesia de San Francisco is one of the oldest churches in the nation, built in 1611. Its adobe walls are more than 39 inches (100 cm) thick; stone blocks are fastened together with leather thongs; and the roof beams are made of cactus. There are two belfries, an unusual feature, and an outside staircase to the towers. Paintings in the church date from the colonial period. The region is also interesting for archaeological finds and for rock paintings in the nearby Loa Valley.

In Santiago, another church named San Francisco was established by Franciscan monks in 1563. The original building was destroyed by an earthquake. Rebuilt in 1683 and later enlarged, the church contains an altar brought from Spain by Pedro de Valdivia.

Franciscan monks established this church in Santiago in the sixteenth century.

A neoclassical cathedral was built in Santiago in the eighteenth century. A Thanksgiving mass is celebrated there each year on September 18. This special ceremony is presided over by the Cardinal Archbishop of Santiago. Special guests include the president of the republic, religious leaders from other denominations, foreign diplomats, and other dignitaries.

Religious Fiestas

Religious festivals and celebrations in some parts of Chile are a mixture of Catholic rites and the older religious practices of native South Americans. Animism—belief in spirits that exist in animals, birds, and other aspects of nature—coexists with Christianity. This kind of combination is called *syncretism*.

The little village of Parinacota, in the far northern highlands near Peru and Bolivia, has been designated a national

People of all ages taking part in a religious festival in the Lakes Region

Frescoes decorate the walls of Parinacota's seventeenth-century church.

monument. It is a ceremonial village. Its forty or fifty houses are abandoned most of the year, but it comes alive at fiesta time. This is common practice in the region, where shepherds are usually away tending their flocks of llamas and alpacas. They return to their village only occasionally, for special celebrations. Parinacota's seventeenth-century church, rebuilt in 1789, is a showpiece of colonial architecture, paintings, and frescoes.

Towering above the villages and high plains are two 19,685-foot (6,000-m) volcanoes, Parinacota and Pomerape. These were once sacred gods to the Aymará shepherds. To this day, annual fiestas honor both the patron saints of mountain villages and the gods of the volcanoes.

La Tirana

Best known of Chile's religious fiestas is a week-long celebration held in La Tirana, near Iquique. It is dedicated to the Virgin of Carmel, Chile's patroness. From 40,000 to 80,000 pilgrims and tourists come to the tiny village in July to worship and enjoy the colorful dances and ceremonies.

The name *La Tirana* means "the tyrant." A bossy woman once managed an inn for travelers at this location. She was nicknamed La Tirana, and both the settlement and the festival came to be known by that name as well. The town is used almost exclusively for this festival, and its houses are closed during the rest of the year. More than a hundred dance troupes gather from all over the altiplano to perform, dressed in masks, bright silk costumes, and shimmering jewels. Women portray virginal maidens; men are disguised as devils.

Dancing goes on night and day, accompanied by music played on drums, whistles, flutes, and native instruments. No alcohol is permitted. The celebration includes prayers, orations, and hymn singing.

Artistic Expression

AS THE SPANISH SETTLED IN CHILE AND INTERMINGLED with the native population, many aspects of life took on a flavor of their own. Just as the Spanish language became distinctly Chilean, so did many songs, dances, costumes, foods, and customs. Other Europeans also brought some of their own tastes into everyday Chilean life.

Chile is a unique blend of European and native South American cultures. Before the twentieth century, European arts had flourished only in the drawing rooms of the rich and powerful. In the 1920s, leadership in artistic achievement shifted to middle-class intellectuals. The poet Gabriela Mistral was a major figure among them.

Opposite: **Dancing the** *cueca*

Gabriela Mistral receiving the Nobel Prize from King Gustaf of Sweden

In recent years, artistic movements have come from a broader section of society. They have also become more international and intercultural. Fashions, cuisine, and entertainment all show North American and, to some extent, Asian influences.

Then there is Easter Island, a part of Chile yet very different from the rest of the country in customs and lifestyle. It is all these different aspects of Chilean life that make Chile such a fascinating country.

Music and Dance

Chileans value the arts of poetry, music, and theater highly. Many professional people take part in performing arts in their spare time.

In colonial times, the Europeans brought their musical instruments to Chile, where they found that the natives had instruments of their own. Spanish guitars melded very well with the native flutes, pipes, whistles, and percussion instruments. Native dances made use of costumes and masks in group performances that imitated the movements of animals. The Spanish introduced religious festivals and pageants and the natives joined in, using their traditional costumes and dance steps.

The national dance of Chile is the *cueca*. Native Chileans didn't care for the formal dance steps used by the Spanish. Chilean dancing was much freer, bolder, and livelier. The *cueca*, which originated in rural areas, is described as an imitation of mating chickens. It has a vigorous one-two rhythm. Guitar and harp music accompanies the dancers, and the audience claps and shouts.

Both dancers wave handkerchiefs in the air as they dance. The aggressive male struts about and shows off while the female acts shy and flirtatious. Costumes for performing the cueca differ from one region to another. In some areas, the dress is simple and the dancers may be barefoot. In others, the women wear elegant dresses and men appear in *huaso* (cowboy) costumes—colorful ponchos and shiny black boots with silver spurs. When the dancers are dressed this way, some observers say the dance is like a cowboy trying to rope a nervous horse.

While women may sometimes play male roles in other Latin American dances, they never do in the cueca. Here the gender roles are very clearly defined—the male is dominant, the female submissive. Various other traditional Latin American dances are also performed at festivals.

The Mapuche people have their own traditional songs, instruments, and dances. So do the people from the northern altiplano and those on the island of Chiloé. In Punta Arenas, traditional songs and dances reflect the ethnic traditions of early

Panpipes are traditional instruments of Chile.

Folk instruments of the Andes include various types of guitars and flutes.

immigrants, particularly the Serbs and Croatians. And on Easter Island, guests are greeted with dances and songs similar to those performed on Polynesian islands.

Young Chilean musicians created a new kind of folk music during the 1960s and 1970s. Called *La Nueva Cancion Chilena* (Chilean New Song), the compositions used traditional folk instruments from the Andes and other regions of South America. Flutes, stringed instruments similar to guitars and ukeleles, drums, and other percussion instruments were used. Words in the folk songs expressed protest against the repressive government, and performers carried the messages to the world. Most of the singers had to leave Chile, and those who remained were blacklisted and persecuted.

New Song records were smuggled into Chile and passed around through an underground during the military regime. The movement has revived and is again popular under Chile's restored democracy.

Violeta Parra

Violeta Parra was born into a musical family. Her parents, her ten brothers and sisters, and her son and daughter were all involved in the arts. Violeta was a singer, songwriter, painter, and sculptor.

A leading member of Chile's New Song movement, she established a center for popular art in Santiago.

Violeta used her work to help people in need, and her folk songs were songs of class struggle. She committed suicide in 1967 and was greatly mourned. Her influence on folk music extended far beyond the borders of Chile. Folksinger Joan Baez made a popular recording of one of Violeta's songs, "Gracias a la Vida."

The Municipal Theater

El Teatro Municipal (the Municipal Theater) in Santiago was built in the 1850s. After it was nearly destroyed by fire in 1870, it was reconstructed by a French architect. The building was again heavily damaged in 1906, by an earthquake. A distinctive feature of the theater is a chandelier with sixty-eight lights that hangs from the cupola.

The Municipal Theater is Chile's major center for the performing arts. National and international troupes perform operas, concerts, and ballets here. Many famous stars have appeared in this theater, from Sarah Bernhardt, a great French actress of the early twentieth century, to today's internationally popular tenor Placido Domingo of Spain.

Painting and Sculpture

Churches and monasteries in Chile have fine collections of South American religious art created during the Spanish colonial period. Most of it did not originate in Chile, however. There was very little religious artistic endeavor in Chile at that time. Paintings and sculpture had to be imported. Since it was very expensive to bring in Spanish works of art, most of the colonial art was ordered from the major cities of Peru.

After independence, Chilean art began to blossom. Local artists branched out into other themes besides religion. They used the Chilean landscape, events in local history, and everyday life and customs as subject matter for their paintings. Local art grew in popularity and importance throughout the nineteenth century. The Chilean Academy of Painting was founded in 1849. Monuments and statues by local sculptors began to appear in Santiago's public areas.

Chilean art produced at the beginning of the 1900s showed the influence of French impressionism. Many serious artists went to Europe to study, and some never came back.

In recent years, Santiago has developed as a cultural center. Artists who have gone abroad are returning home to work. Chilean art is developing in new and imaginative directions.

A project called the Art-Industry Encounter encourages experimentation and creativity. The state and private enterprise are working together to promote new thinking about art. Traditional forms of expression are supported, but fresh and unusual approaches are also stimulated. Fine artists are encouraged to go into factories and industries. There, with the help of factory workers, they create sculptures using many kinds of materials.

Museums

Santiago has many fine museums. Their collections include pre-Columbian art, colonial religious art, natural history, and historical artifacts from Santiago. One museum features steam

The Fine Arts Museum in Santiago

engines. The Museo de Arte Popular Americano houses a large collection of folk art from both North and South America. The archaeology of Easter Island is exhibited and explained at the Museo Iglesia de la Merced.

Chilean landscapes and seascapes are on display in Valparaíso at the Museo Municipal de Bellas Artes. Valparaíso has a Naval Museum and another museum where naval models are on display. The city also honors Chile's most famous poets in two museums. Museo La Sebastiana is the former home of Pablo Neruda, and Casa Mistral is an exhibit based on the life and work of Gabriela Mistral.

A fascinating museum in Valdivia is housed in an old mansion. It has three sections—one devoted to the Spanish colonial era, one to the German immigration to the region, and one to the Mapuche people. The Museo Regional de la Araucanía in

Temuco has a Mapuche library and exhibits commemorating the Mapuche culture and the struggle between the Mapuches and the Spaniards during the colonial period.

Crafts

The Mapuche people are masters of several kinds of arts and crafts. Silversmiths fashion earrings, pins, necklaces, and headbands. The university in Temuco lends encouragement to this traditional craft. Weavers create ponchos, rugs, and bedspreads out of handspun sheep's wool. They use natural dyes to make bright colors.

Handmade baskets are used in the home, in fishing, and in farming. Some of the Mapuches make their own musical instruments; others carve animal horns and antlers into cups, spoons, and small figures of birds and animals.

Handcrafted model boats

On the island of Chiloé, artisans are famous for their hand-knitted woolen goods, colored with natural dyes. They are also known for their basketwork, mats, and ornamental figures, and for their handcrafted model boats.

Northern Chilean natives weave alpaca and llama hair into textiles for clothing, decorative wall hangings, blankets, and rugs. Residents of the Atacama use cactus wood for carvings and to make native flutes, panpipes, and small stringed instruments.

A famous black pottery with white patterns is used to form figures of humans and other creatures in Chile's Central Valley. Terra-cotta dishes and utensils are made in Pomaire, west of Santiago. In Santiago and Los Angeles, nuns of the Comunidad de Santa Clara create highly decorated pieces of pottery. The work of this religious order has been famous since colonial times.

A bright blue gemstone called lapis lazuli is set with copper or silver to make jewelry and decorations. Most of the world's lapis mining is done in only two countries— Chile and Afghanistan.

A brooch made of lapis lazuli and silver

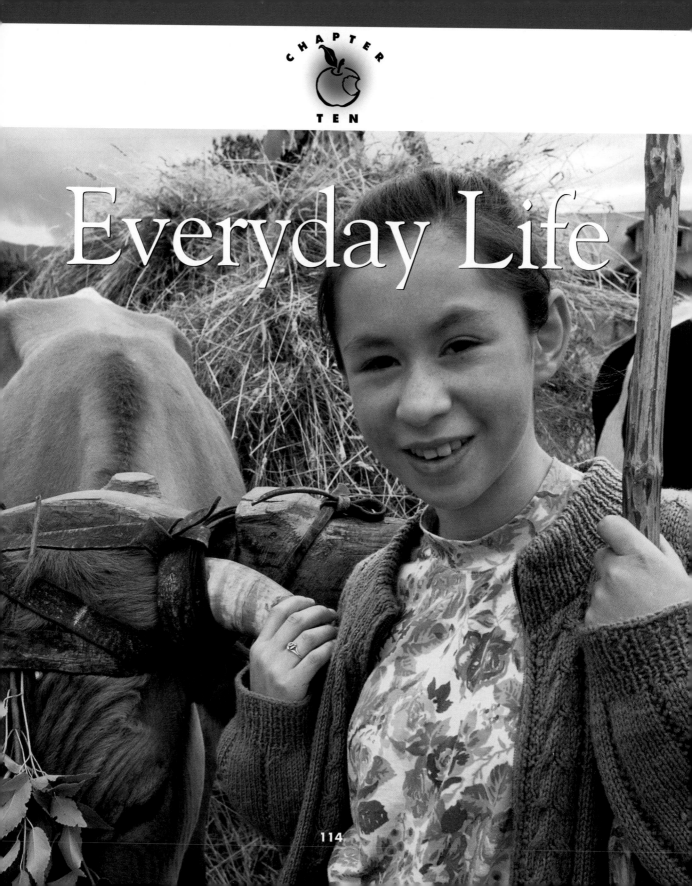

CHAPTER TEN

Everyday Life

I N CHILE, AS IN OTHER COUNTRIES, EVERYDAY LIFE FOR children differs greatly depending on where the children live and who their parents are. An Aymará boy who lives in the mountains in northern Chile may spend a lot of time with his father, taking care of llamas and other livestock. His sister probably learns to crochet when she is very young and helps her mother make brightly colored scarves and caps to sell in a nearby market.

Opposite: **A Mapuche girl helping to manage livestock**

An Aymará family at home

In the Central Valley, many people work on farms, and the children help out at busy times of the year. The family may own their own land, or they may work on large farms as share-croppers or employees. Most rural people are poor and live in small houses. Adobe houses with tile or thatched roofs are seen in the north. In regions where trees are plentiful, the houses are made of wood.

In some of the villages in the Chilean Archipelago, the children almost never see a stranger. There are no roads leading to some of these villages; the only transport is by boat. Many houses in this region are built on stilts at the edge of water.

In some areas houses are built on stilts.

Nearly half of the children in Chile, on the other hand, live in the Metropolitan Region of Santiago. Theirs is a city life. They live among modern steel-and-glass skyscrapers and Spanish-style buildings with patios and red-tile roofs. There are plenty of trees, parks, and gardens.

A shopping center in downtown Santiago

Rich and Poor

The old class system of colonial Chile was based on ancestry. Upper-class people were all Spanish, the middle class were mestizos, and the lower class were mostly natives. It has not changed a great deal since then, except that today it is wealth, not ancestry, that determines a person's status. Most of the few really wealthy people are of European descent, however, and the poorest people are generally either mestizo or descended from Chilean natives.

Santiago is where most of the nation's rich people live. New suburbs have appeared in the foothills east of Santiago, complete with shopping malls, supermarkets, and bus lines. Children of wealthy parents live in spacious apartments or in houses with big lawns and fenced-in gardens.

Middle-class families—doctors, businesspeople, and government workers—also have comfortable city homes, somewhat less luxurious than those of their richer neighbors. The poorest city families usually live in tiny, run-down shacks in crowded slums.

During summer, everyone who can manage to do so heads for the beaches. Chile's long, thin shape makes the Pacific beaches easily accessible for most people. Wealthy families make excursions to the mountains in the south for skiing. But many Chilean children have never been in the mountains and have never touched snow or seen snow fall.

In summer, people head for the beaches.

Education

Schoolchildren in uniform

Chilean children are required to go to school for eight years. There are free public schools, as well as some private ones. In the remote rural areas, it is very hard for some children to get to a school, but most do make it. More than nine out of ten adult Chileans can read and write.

All schoolchildren in Chile wear uniforms. The uniforms vary slightly according to the students' age. Young boys are dressed in white shirts, gray slacks, blue jackets, and black shoes. Young girls wear blue jumpers over white shirts, with blue socks and black shoes. At recess, many schoolboys play soccer while the girls jump rope and play *bolitas* (marbles).

Preschool programs are financed by the government. The number of children in these programs has increased a great deal in recent years. Still, there are only enough programs for a few of Chile's small children.

National Holidays in Chile

New Year's Day	January 1
Holy Week	March/April (date varies)
Labor Day	May 1
Naval Battle of Iquique	May 21
Corpus Christi	May 30
Saint Peter & Saint Paul's Day	June 29
Assumption	August 15
Military Coup of 1973	September 11
Independence Day	September 18
Armed Forces Day	September 19
Columbus Day	October 12
All Saints' Day	November 1
Immaculate Conception	December 8
Christmas Day	December 25

Higher education got an early start in this country. The University of Chile was established in 1842, in Santiago. The university was a world pioneer in coeducation when it admitted women in 1877. Many new universities have been created in recent years. Today Chile has a few dozen universities, as well as scores of training institutes and technical schools.

Women in Chile

Women make up nearly one-third of the workforce in Chile. In many families, both parents work outside the home. Wealthy and middle-class families hire servants to care for their children.

Chilean women are active in voting and in political movements but, so far, not many have run for elected office. They

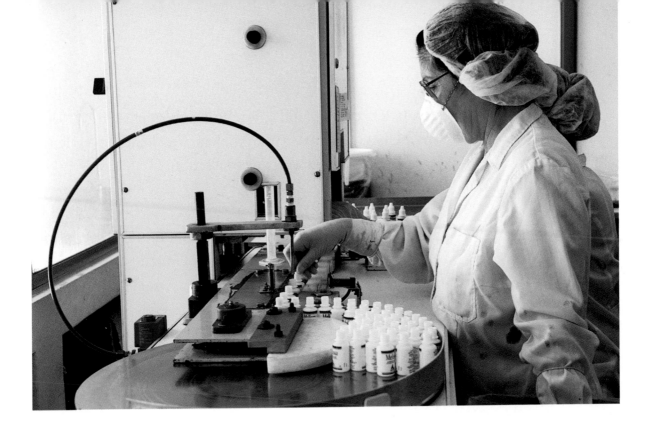

are well represented in the professions, however, especially in dentistry. Half of Chile's dentists are women.

President Frei's cabinet included three women—the Minister of Justice, the Minister of National Heritage, and the National Secretary for Women's Affairs (Sernam). Sernam was created to increase the involvement of women in government and to coordinate public policies that benefit women. Chile was a signer of the United Nations Convention for the elimination of discrimination against women.

Among other commitments, Sernam has organized a child-care program for the children of women who do seasonal work. This office helps women who are the sole support of their families in such areas as health care, job opportunities, housing, and legal aid. It has established women's-rights information centers and job-training programs. In addition, Sernam is concerned with problems of domestic violence, teenage pregnancy, and cancer detection.

Social Welfare

Chile established a government program of social security in 1924, more than ten years before the United States started a social security program. A health-care system was started in the 1950s that provided free care to workers and poor people. A decade later, the health system expanded to include preventive care for babies and mothers.

Everyday clothing in Chile is similar to clothing worn in most of the world today.

Unfortunately, hard times made it difficult for the government to pay for these programs, and the military government of the 1970s and 1980s abandoned support for many of them. Presidents Aylwin and Frei have increased allotments for health care and education, but government support of social security is still nonexistent.

Clothing

As a rule, Chileans dress much like people in the United States, Canada, and Europe. In fact, everyday clothing is becoming quite similar in most of the world. People wear regional or traditional costumes only for special celebrations or ceremonies.

One of these special occasions is a rodeo. *Huasos* (Chilean cowboys) dress for rodeos in large, flat-topped hats, brightly colored sashes, ponchos, fringed leather pants, and big black boots. Araucanian women ordinarily wear distinctive hand-woven shawls and chunky silver jewelry.

Top left: **People wear traditional costumes for special occasions, such as this rodeo.**

Top right: **A Mapuche healer in traditional attire**

Food

Chile's unusual geography, with altitudes ranging from sea level to high mountains and climates from subtropical to sub-Antarctic, has produced a great variety of native foods. Nature provides dozens of kinds of fish and shellfish, bountiful crops of fruits and vegetables, and grazing lands for ranch-fed

Celebrations

National holiday celebrations are rare in Chile. The most important one, Independence Day, is observed on September 18 with parades, kite-flying, dancing, eating and drinking, and general merriment. But most festivals are regional affairs.

Chileans like to entertain family and friends with parties at home. Quite often, the party will be an important social event with lots of guests, called an *asado*. Literally, *asado* means "roast," and that is exactly what is served. An asado is not just a simple backyard cookout with hamburgers or hot dogs, however. Huge, elaborate roasts of meat are cooked slowly, outdoors, for these gala occasions.

When a person dies, people gather together to socialize. The occasion is a celebration in honor of a person's life, and food and drink are served. Weddings are another good reason for parties, which often go on for three days.

extensively to make the famous Chilean wines, but there are plenty left over to eat fresh from the vine.

Mote con huesillos, made of dried peaches with cooked cracked wheat, is a traditional Chilean dessert. Many other desserts use an ingredient called *manjar*. It is made of condensed milk boiled down to a thick, gooey, caramel concoction. Manjar is spread between layers of cake or filo pastry, or eaten simply as a topping on bread.

Coffee, tea, and Chilean wines are the popular beverages. If their work schedule permits it, some Chileans eat a large and leisurely dinner in early afternoon, a small meal of tea or coffee with sandwiches and sweets at five or six, then a light supper later on.

Entertainment and Sports

With mountains and seashores at almost every doorstep, Chileans have great opportunities for outdoor recreation—fishing, boating, hiking, and skiing. Family outings often include these pleasures. Movies, plays, ballets, and operas are popular entertainment, especially in the cities. Chileans also like to attend sporting events, such as horse races, tennis matches, and basketball games. Horse shows, too, are popular, and Chile has produced world record–holders in equestrian high jumping.

But one sport outshines all the rest. *Fútbol*, or soccer, is Chile's national sport. Children start playing it at an early age, and adults are passionate about it. They crowd the stadiums or sit glued to their television sets for important matches.

The entire nation was thrilled when Chile's soccer team qualified to compete for the World Cup in June 1998, in France. It was Chile's seventh appearance in World Cup matches, and the nation hosted the games in 1962, but this was the team's first participation since 1982.

A 1998 World Cup match against Cameroon

Timeline

Chilean History		World History
	2500 B.C.	Egyptians build the Pyramids and Sphinx in Giza.
	563 B.C.	Buddha is born in India.
	A.D. 313	The Roman emperor Constantine recognizes Christianity.
	610	The prophet Muhammad begins preaching a new religion called Islam.
	1054	The Eastern (Orthodox) and Western (Roman) Churches break apart.
	1066	William the Conqueror defeats the English in the Battle of Hastings.
	1095	Pope Urban II proclaims the First Crusade.
	1215	King John seals the Magna Carta.
	1300s	The Renaissance begins in Italy.
	1347	The Black Death sweeps through Europe.
	1453	Ottoman Turks capture Constantinople, conquering the Byzantine Empire.
Incas from Peru settled in Chile, conquering Indians in northern Chile.	Late 1400s	
	1492	Columbus arrives in North America.
Ferdinand Magellan, a Portuguese navigator, is the first European to sight Chile.	1520	1500s The Reformation leads to the birth of Protestantism.
Diego de Almagro leads the first Spanish expedition to explore Chile.	1535–1537	
Pedro de Valdivia conquers Chile.	1540	
Araucanian Indian uprising.	1553–1558	
Pope Paul V authorizes war against the Araucanians.	1609	
Bourbon reforms give Chile greater independence from the Viceroyalty of Peru.	1759–1796	1776 The Declaration of Independence is signed.
		1789 The French Revolution begins.

Chilean History

Criollo leaders of Santiago declare independence from Spain.	1810
National Congress is established.	1811
Spanish troops from Peru reconquer Chile at the Battle of Rancagua.	1814
Troops led by Bernardo O'Higgins and General José de San Martín defeat the Spanish in the Battle of Chacabuco.	1817
Declaration of independence from Spain.	1818
Period of civil wars.	1818–1830
Slavery is abolished.	1823
The Portales Constitution is adopted.	1833
Chile wages war with Peru and Bolivia, in the War of the Pacific; Chile's victory is sealed with the Treaty of Ancón.	1879–1883
Civil war breaks out.	1891
Massacre of Iquique: Hundreds of men, women, and children are killed by the army.	1907
New Constitution provides separation of church and state, the right of workers to form labor unions, and the promise to care for the welfare of all citizens.	1925
Salvador Allende is elected president; many leftist reforms are enacted.	1970
General Augusto Pinochet leads coup; Pinochet's cruel military dictatorship is established.	1973
A new Constitution provides for a gradual return to democracy; the military government continues to restrict the rights of its opponents.	1980
Transition to democracy begins with presidency of Patricio Aylwin Azócar; Pinochet remains head of the armed forces.	1990
Aylwin is succeeded by Eduardo Frei Ruiz-Tagle. Chile is the first South American country invited to join the North American Free Trade Agreement (NAFTA).	1994
Approval of Chile's NAFTA membership is delayed by opposition in the U.S. Congress.	1996

World History

1865	The American Civil War ends.
1914	World War I breaks out.
1917	The Bolshevik Revolution brings Communism to Russia.
1929	Worldwide economic depression begins.
1939	World War II begins, following the German invasion of Poland.
1957	The Vietnam War starts.
1989	The Berlin Wall is torn down as Communism crumbles in Eastern Europe.
1996	Bill Clinton is reelected U.S. president.

Fast Facts

Official name: *República de Chile* (Republic of Chile)

Capital: Santiago

Official language: Spanish

Valparaíso

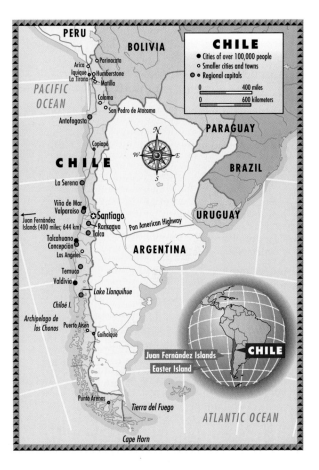

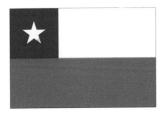

Flag of Chile

La Serena Valley

Official religion:	Roman Catholicism
Year of founding:	1818 (liberation from Spain)
Founder:	Bernardo O'Higgins (*El Libertador*)
National anthem:	*Himno Nacional de Chile* ("National Song of Chile")
Government:	Multiparty republic
Chief of state:	President
Head of government:	President
Area:	292,135 square miles (756,571 sq km)
Latitude and longitude of geographic center:	30° 00' South, 71° 00' West
Land and water borders:	Peru to the north, South Pole to the south, Bolivia and Argentina to the east, Pacific Ocean to the west
Highest elevation:	Nevado Ojos del Salado, 22,566 feet (6,878 m)
Lowest elevation:	Pacific Ocean, sea level
Average temperatures:	43°F (6°C) in Punta Arenas (far south), 63°F (17°C) in Antofagasta (far north)
Average precipitation:	From 0.5 inches (1.3 cm) in Antofagasta in the north to 200 inches (508 cm) at the Strait of Magellan in the south. In central Chile, the average rainfall is 14 inches (36 cm).
National population (1998 est.):	14,787,781

Easter Island statue

Currency

Population of largest cities (1995 est.):

Santiago	4,295,593
Concepción	350,268
Viña del Mar	322,220
Valparaíso	282,168

Famous landmarks:

▶ *Easter Island* is the site of 300 mysterious, huge statues of human forms

▶ *Iglesia de San Francisco* (Chiu-Chiu), built in 1611, is one of Chile's oldest churches.

▶ *Museo La Sebastiana* (Valparaíso) is the former home of poet Pablo Neruda.

▶ *Museo Regional de la Araucanía* (Temuco) features exhibits and a library devoted to the Mapuche culture.

▶ *Museo de Arte Popular Americano* (Santiago) houses a collection of folk art from North and South America.

▶ *Torres del Paine National Park* has spectacular scenery and abundant wildlife.

▶ *Valley of the Moon* (near San Pedro de Atacama) is a landscape of strange-looking salt, gypsum, and clay formations.

Industry: Chile's most important industries are mining (primarily copper), foodstuffs, fish processing, iron and steel, wood and wood products, transport equipment, cement, and textiles. Agriculture (including fishing and forestry) accounts for about 8% of the GDP; industry, 33%; and services, 59% (1995 est.).

Currency: Chile's basic monetary unit is the peso. In early 2000, U.S.$1 = 517 pesos.

Young Chileans

Salvador Allende

System of weights and measures: Metric system

Literacy rate (1995 est.): 95.2 %

Common Spanish words and phrases:

¡Hola!	Hello!
¿Qué tal?	How are you?
¿Qué hora es?	What time is it?
¡Adiós!	Goodbye!
Buenos días.	Good day *or* Hello.
Buenas noches.	Goodnight.
Por favor	Please
Gracias.	Thank-you.
De nada.	You're welcome.
¿Habla usted inglés?	Do you speak English?

Famous Chileans:

Salvador Allende Gossens   (1908–1973)
President

Gabriela Mistral   (1889–1957)
Poet, Nobel Prize–winner

Pablo Neruda   (1904–1973)
Poet, Nobel Prize–winner

Bernardo O'Higgins   (1778–1842)
Founder

Violeta Parra   (1917–1967)
Musician, artist

Augusto Pinochet Ugarte   (1915–)
Military dictator

To Find Out More

Books

▶ Dwyer, Christopher. *Chile, Major World Nations*. New York: Chelsea House Publishers, 1997.

▶ Galvin, Irene Flum. *Chile: Journey to Freedom* (formerly titled *Chile: Land of Poets and Patriots*). Parsippany, NJ: Silver Burdett Press, 1996.

▶ Haverstock, Nathan A. *Chile in Pictures*. Visual Geography Series. Minneapolis: Lerner Publications, 1988.

▶ Hughes, Brenda. *Folk Tales from Chile*. Library of Folklore. New York: Hippocrene Books, 1998.

Websites

▶ **Chile**
http://www.ddg.com/LIS/aurelia/chile.htm
A variety of facts on the country, including history, geography, climate, population, economy, government, and tourism.

▶ **The CIA World Factbook 1999**
http://www.odci.gov/cia/publications/factbook/ci.html
Displays updated information on and maps of the country, including facts on geography, people, government, economy, communications, transportation, and more.

▶ GORP—Great Outdoor
Recreation Pages
http://www.gorp.com/gorp/location/
latamer/chile/chil_pks.htm
*Includes information on national parks,
national reserves, and other attractions
of Chile.*

▶ Travel Photography Online:
Central and South America
http://www.travelphoto.net/photos/
english/chile/E1.HTM
*Many beautiful photos of Chile,
Argentina, and a variety of other
countries.*

Organizations and Embassies

▶ **Embassy of Chile**
1732 Massachusetts Ave. N.W.
Washington, DC 20090-1981
(202) 785-1746

▶ **Chilean Consulate**
866 United Nations Plaza
New York, NY 10017-1822
(212) 980-3366

Index

Page numbers in *italics* indicate illustrations.

Meet the Author

SYLVIA McNAIR was born in Korea and believes she inherited a love of travel from her missionary parents. She grew up in Vermont. After graduating from Oberlin College, she held a variety of jobs, married, had four children, and settled in the Chicago area. She now lives in Evanston, Illinois. She is the author of several travel guides and more than a dozen books for young people published by Children's Press. McNair has traveled in more than forty countries and in all fifty of the United States.

"I first visited Chile on a cruise ship, sailing through the archipelago and taking side trips to several national parks. The scenery in this country is incredible. In almost every corner of Chile, a person can see mountains and still be only a short distance from the Pacific Ocean. On later visits, I saw

the farmlands and groves and vineyards of the Central Valley, then the deserts in the north.

"Chile's geography lured me first. Then, as I learned about the country's history and met some of the people, I became interested in learning more about it. One of the best things about my work is that I get the chance to learn about things that arouse my curiosity.

"I love to travel and I love writing about faraway places. I relive my travels as I write. I remember the sights and sounds and smells, the exotic foods I tasted, the people I've met from many parts of the world.

"I hope this book will make some of you readers curious to learn more about Chile, as well as many other places around the world."

Photo Credits